# Leading the Little Ones to Mary

*by*

SISTER MARY LELIA, S.S.N.D.

*Ninth Printing, 2008*

AY SHORE, NEW YORK, 11706-8993

*Designed by John Harding*

*Imprimi Potest:*   FRANK A. SETZER, S.M.M.,

                                        *Provincial Superior.*

*Nihil Obstat:*   MARTIN J. HEALY, S.T.D.,

                                        *Censor Librorum*

*Imprimatur:*   WALTER PHILIP KELLENBERG, D.D.,

                                        *Bishop of Rockville C*

7/1/'59

*ISBN 0-910984-13-1*

# CONTENTS

# PREFACE

This Marian program has but one purpose, to imbue the little ones with a genuine devotion to Mary. Therefore, it is not intended as a pious practice for May or October. It is rather a copying of Mary—a way of life. It is the De Montfort Method simplified for young minds.

There are sixteen series in all. If begun in the fall, the entire series can be covered in a school year. A day or two should elapse between talks to allow time for the children to assimilate the matter. During this time they are gently and joyously reminded of the little practices by slogans which are a tiny digest of something spiritually worthwhile—something the children can cherish in the memory through the years. The teacher's encouraging commendations are also a spur to greater effort as—I saw a little Mary doing something kind today. Our Lady will be looking for her Marios at Mass on Sunday. How many copied Mary over the weekend? etc.

It is not expected that the children retain all the story facts. The real object will be attained if they imbibe a holy and happy love for their holy Mother and can grasp, according to each one's capacity, the meaning of the consecration they make so frequently.

According to the principle, "no impression without its corresponding expression," the children must participate in these talks. This they can do by the comments they give. Thus the matter becomes their own. In this way, the teacher gets a fair estimate of the comprehension of her little listeners.

The program has been widely used in first, second, and third grades with gratifying results. Teachers have enthusiastically reported about the appreciation evinced by their eager little groups.

Mothers and teachers truly in love with Our Lady will be ingenious in including all visual and other aids available in the guidance of their little Marys and Marios to our Holy Mother.

*The Author*

# LEADING THE LITTLE ONES TO MARY

*By* SISTER MARY LELIA, S.S.N.D.

CHAPTER I

## MARY

*First Talk*

Once upon a time there was a certain little girl. God and His angels used to look down from heaven to see this dear little girl. They were so pleased with her. They could hardly take their eyes off her.

They loved to see her pray. And they liked the way she ran when her mother called. She helped at home, too. In school she always listened. She did not miss a thing. There were so many good things she did. (Let children supplement.) All this pleased God and His angels.

Now, can you guess who this little girl was? Yes, it was Mary. God loved her very much. All the angels loved her. And so do we. Don't we? Well, then, let us tell Mary that we, too, love her. (Have children fold their hands and each one whisper her little secret to Mary.)

(This first talk may be reviewed the next day before going on to the second point.)

*Second Talk*

Who was the little girl we have been talking about? Why did God and all His angels keep looking down at her? (Get children's comments. Ask: "Where is Mary now?") Yes, in heaven. And now she is looking down, too, along with God and the angels. Do

**LITTLE MARY AND LITTLE MARIO**

you want to know why? Well, they are looking for little girls who act just like Mary. And when Our Lady sees a little girl acting that way, she has a special name for her. She calls her "little Mary." Isn't that lovely?

(Where there are boys in the classes, the teacher can insert.) . . . And when Our Lady sees a little girl or a little boy acting that way she has a lovely name for each of them. She calls the girl little Mary. And she calls her boy Mario, my knight, my page, lieutenant, scout, etc. (as the teacher may see fit).

Our Lady wants many, many little Marys. She can't have enough. The more she can find the better. Do you think she finds many? Oh, yes, I know some right here in this room. But couldn't we have more? Wouldn't it be lovely if all our angels could say, "This room is filled with little Marys"?

How many want to be little Marys? Very well, all we have to do is to copy Mary.

> Play like Mary
> Pray like Mary
> Help like Mary
> Obey like Mary
> Share like Mary

But we must tell her about it. Let us fold our hands and each little girl talk to Our Lady. Be sure to ask her to help you to keep your promise.

(Very slowly say the following aloud for the children. They will follow in thought.) Dear Holy Mary, I know you are looking for little Marys. I do want to be a little Mary. I promise you that I will

                    act like you
                    pray like you
                    play like you
                    help like you
                    obey like you
                    share like you

Please help me to keep my promise.

(Review the foregoing by questions for the length of time it seems necessary without boring the children.)

*Third Talk*

We told Holy Mary that we want to be little Marys. What does that mean? (Let children talk.)

To be little Marys we must do something else. There is something else that Mary wants. She wants each little girl to belong to her. And besides that, she wants everything we do—everything. She wants all the good things we do

                    at home
                    at school
                    in church
                    on the playground

We must give her everything. Then we shall really belong to her.

If we do all this, our angels will say, "Now all these little Marys really belong to God's Mother. When Communion Day comes she will be so glad to give them her little Jesus. And dear Jesus will be glad to come to them because they are little Marys."

So now we shall tell Our Lady another nice surprise. Let us fold our hands and mean just what we say.

*Consecration* — Holy Mary I want to belong to you. I give you my whole self and all the good things I do,

> at home
> at school
> in church
> on the playground

My Mother, I am all yours, and all I do belongs to you. (Review and get pupils' comments, using as many days as you see fit.)

## Fourth Talk

Now we are little Marys. We belong to Mary. From now on, no matter what good things we do, Mary will take them. She will touch them up and make them look nicer. Then she will give them to our dear Lord. (Renew the consecration.)

(To make this series of talks bear fruit, the children will need little reminders now and then. Gentle remarks such as these will help:)

I saw a little Mary (or Mario) do something very kind today.

Our Lady will be looking for her little Marys in church on Sunday.

How many little Marys copied Our Lady over the week-end?

I see some little Marys doing very neat work in their books, etc.

*Suggested Reading*

"Treatise on True Devotion to the Blessed Virgin" by St. Louis De Montfort: Montfort Publications, Bay Shore, N.Y. 11706.

"True Devotion to Mary" (adapted) by Eddie Doherty: Montfort Publications, Bay Shore, N.Y. 11706.

"Queen of All Hearts" (magazine): Montfort Fathers, Bay Shore, N.Y. 11706.

CHAPTER II

# MARY AT HOME

*First Talk*

(Have children repeat their consecration to Mary. Then show a picture of Mary with St. Anne.)

This is holy Mary with St. Anne. St. Joachim was Mary's father. Anne and Joachim loved their dear child more than anyone can tell. When Mary went to fetch a jar of water or do some other errand they always missed her. But as soon as Anne heard Mary coming in she would say, "Here comes our darling."

You see Mary helped a lot to make the home a happy place. She made her mother and father happy. And I am sure she made her angel happy, too.

Now don't you think Our Lady wants her little Marys to copy her? (Children's comments.) How fine it would be if each mother could say, "My, how I miss my little girl when she is not at home. I am glad when week-ends come and I can have her with me." (More comments.)

**MARY AT HOME**

Well, let us fold our hands and tell Our Lady that we will try to be like her. (Renew consecration.)

*Second Talk*

How did St. Anne feel when Mary was not at home? What did she say when she heard Mary coming in? What kind of home did Mary help to make? I wonder what it was that she did? (Children's comments.)

Yes, Mary did all those nice things. She came right away when her mother called her. She put away her clothes and toys, etc. She jumped out of bed when she was called. And she was not fussy about eating what was good for her. Her mother did not have to ask her to set the table. Mary offered to do it. And here is something lovely: Mary always did all these things with a sweet smile. Why did Mary do all this? (Children's comments.) Yes, to please God. St. Anne must have been very happy about all that. But what about Mary's angel? (Children's comments.)

Let us pick out all the nice things Mary did and each one ask herself, "How many of these things am I doing?" See if we can guess the best thing of all. This may help you. It tells how Mary did things. (If children cannot guess, tell them.) Mary did all with a smile. We want to remember this. So we shall write it on the blackboard. (Have the children whisper the slogan many times.) Do you think we can act like that? (Renew consecration.)

## Third Talk

Tell me some of the things Mary did at home. Were they just the same things that any child does? Who can tell me the slogan?

Mary had neighbors, too. Some of the children were her friends. How do you think she treated her little friends? (Children's comments.)

Some of Mary's little neighbors were not always good. They did not obey their mothers. Some told lies and called names. And some made fun of people. These children copied from naughty boys and girls.

The mothers told their children to see how Mary acted. And do you know, many of these boys and girls really began to copy holy Mary, because she always did the better thing. They all loved her for that.

I wonder if we little Marys always do the better thing? It would be sad if we copied bad children. That would be pleasing the bad angel. We don't ever want to do that. We want to please Our Lady. And how can we do that? (Children's comment.)

So we shall write another thing about Mary. What shall it be? Slogan: *Mary always did the better thing.* (Have children take turns reading it.) (Renew consecration.)

### Suggested Reading

"St. Anne, Cult and Shrines" by Myles V. Ronan: P. J. Kenedy, New York.

"Simple Life of Our Lady" by A Sister of Notre Dame: B. Herder Co., St. Louis, Mo.

"The Secret of Mary Explained to Children" Montfort Publications, Bay Shore, N.Y. 11706

# CHAPTER III

# MARY AT CHURCH

*First Talk*

(Any suitable picture.)

The church that Mary went to was called the Temple. Let us close our eyes for a minute and imagine we see Mary in the Temple. Show me how you think she looked when she prayed, Linda. What were God and the angels doing? (Comments.)

Mary never forgot that the Temple was God's House. And she never forgot how to act in that holy place. Even when other children forgot, Mary kept on acting like a dear child of God. She paid no attention to such girls and boys. Mary wanted to get God's blessing. And we know that she got more blessings than anyone else ever got. We know something lovely about Mary—she is full of grace. So we want to get all the grace we can. And the best way to get it is to act like Mary when we are in church. Suppose we say, *"I will copy Mary in church."* (Post slogan on the blackboard.) Renew consecration.

*Second Talk*

(Suitable picture.)

What did Mary remember when she was in the Temple? And who remembers the slogan? Now Mary's church was not like our church. It was God's House but still it was not as holy as ours. The Jews did not have our dear Lord on the altar as we do. Now you know why our churches are holier than the Temple.

**MARY IN THE CHURCH**

Can you tell me why our Lord is in the Tabernacle? Yes, and He loves to hear us tip-toeing in to pay Him a visit. Does anyone else feel glad when we do that? Yes, indeed. Mary is happy about it. She wants all her children to love the place where our Lord stays and waits for us. Mary wants them to get into the habit of dropping in to talk to our dear Lord. (Comments.)

I wonder what are some of the things children might pray for? (Comments.) But you must not forget to pray for yourself so that you will grow up to be a real child of God. And you must not forget to ask God to help you to be just what He wants. Maybe He wants some of you to be Sisters. We need many more Sisters, and priests, too. So we have to pray for these things. God loves to give us graces and blessings, but He wants us to ask for them. And let us remember to copy Mary when we pray. (Consecration.)

*Third Talk*

(Picture of child at prayer.)

Where else do we pray besides in church? (List the replies as the children give them.) There are many places, aren't there? God and Our Lady want little Marys to get the habit of praying often.

But there is one thing we usually do before we pray. Can you guess? Yes, and the Sign of the Cross is surely a strong prayer. We make it often, but sometimes we forget how strong it is. And one or two of Mary's children forget just how to make it.

Well, here is a little story. One day a little girl

named Bernadette was going over a field. All of a sudden she saw a beautiful Lady. The Lady was so beautiful that the little girl could hardly look up to her. She was really scared. It was our Blessed Mother, but Bernadette did not know that. She pulled out her rosary and began to make the Sign of the Cross. And what do you think? Our holy Mother raised her eyes to heaven and began to make it, too. Bernadette said that as long as she lived she would never forget how Our Lady made that holy Sign. So when we little Marys make that Sign, whom shall we copy? Yes, and let us make it now. (Consecration.)

*Fourth Talk*

(Suitable picture.)

Is there any time when we have to go to church? Yes, and Mary wants to see us there every Sunday, even in vacation. She knows that Mass is the greatest thing on earth. And she is disappointed if she does not see us there. This is why.

In the Mass the priest says the holy words, and right away our Lord comes down on the altar. The priest offers Him to God the Father for us. And our Lord does it, too. The Father is pleased with this Gift, and gives us all the blessings and graces we need.

But if we want these blessings we must pay attention to the priest and keep with him. Then we will be offering the Mass with the priest.

Our angels go to Mass with us. How good it would be if they could say, "These little Marys know how to share in the Mass. They know it is the greatest thing on earth. You won't catch them missing any blessings."

When we go home after Mass we carry blessings home with us. That's why the family that goes to Mass is blessed. So now I am sure we will be careful to please Jesus and Mary at Mass. (Renew consecration.)

*Suggested Reading*

"Story of Mary, Mother of God" by Catherine Beebe: Bruce Pub. Co., Milwaukee, Wis.

"Girlhood of Mary" by Marian Brunowe: Cathedral Library Association, New York.

"Life of the Blessed Virgin in Pictures" by Father O'Brien: Extension Press, Chicago, Ill.

CHAPTER IV

# MARY AT SCHOOL

*First Talk*

(Expose a picture of the Presentation.)

When Mary was a very little girl, her mother and father took her to the Temple. There they offered her up to God. They gave God their best gift. (Have children identify the characters in the picture in answer to questions.)

This temple was God's House. Next to it was a school. Mary was to stay and go to this school with other children. She was happy to be near God's House. Do you know why? Yes, she loved it. And she was glad to go to school.

St. Anne and St. Joachim kissed Mary good-bye and went home. They did not have to worry about their child. They knew their darling would always do

**MARY AT SCHOOL**

her very best. Wasn't that lovely? That means just the same as Mary always did the _____. (Let children finish the known slogan.) And as I look into many bright eyes I can see that you want to do the same. Then let us say our prayer to Mary. (Consecration.)

## Second Talk

(Review the Presentation by questions.) How do you think Mary acted in school? (Comments.) Yes, you see Mary was a good listener. She never missed anything the teacher said. And of course a child like that pleases God. She pleases her own mother because her reports are good. She makes her teacher happy, too. And all the while, see how much she is learning.

We have many children in here that copy Mary just like that. Now if everyone acted that way, each little chair in here would hold a real little Mary. Our angels could then say, "These children never miss a thing."

What did we say about Mary in the beginning of this story? (Comments.) (Elicit the slogan: *Mary was a good listener.* Have it repeated.) God gave each of us two wonderful ears. They are God's gifts. Let us use them the way Mary did. (Renew consecration.)

## Third Talk

Who can tell me the slogan about Mary in school? The teachers and the children in the Temple school must have loved Mary. She got along so nicely with her little friends. Do you think she ever told tales? And how about sharing? (Comments.)

Mary was always a help to her teacher. Can you tell how she might have helped? Well, now, that is just what we little Marys must be doing, too. We must copy Our Lady, even in school. If we act like her we are always right. We shall have a lot to give her. And we know what happens to our good deeds when she takes them in her holy hands, don't we? Did you like the story of Mary at school? Tell me some of the parts you like best. (Comments.)

And how grand it is that Our Lady is now in heaven looking down on us. It makes her happy to see us getting better and better each day. (Renew the consecration.)

*Suggested Reading*

"Life of the Blessed Virgin" by Daniel Lord, S.J.: Wm. J. Hirten Co., Inc., New York.

"Saints Upon a Time" by Joan Windham: Sheed & Ward, New York.

CHAPTER V

# MARY AT PLAY

*First Talk*

We have been talking about how Mary acted at home, in church, and at school. Do you think her school had a place to play? I wonder with whom she played and how she played. (Comments.) Yes, Mary played fair. She was a good loser in games, too. Mary liked to see all her playmates happy.

Even when Mary played with her little neighbors at home she was just the same. The children would run to Mary to play with her. All the mothers were

**MARY AT PLAY**

happy to see their children playing with Anne's little darling. And I think the mothers found the children getting better and better. What about that?

Tell me some of the things that made them more like Mary? (List the acts. Have several pupils read them.) (Renew the consecration.)

*Second Talk*

Does Mary like to see us play? Of course she does. When she came to the three children of Fatima, they were playing. They must have been acting like her. We must be sure to play like Mary. Then we can offer her our play to give to God. We will play fair — be good losers — and listen to the counsellors or the game teachers.

Suppose there is a child all by herself that no one cares about? What should we do about it? (Comments.) Yes, our Blessed Lady would like that.

Sometimes we have to play indoors. If mother has a headache, or tired daddy is reading, or someone is asleep, what then? (Comments.) That's lovely and kind. Mary will surely smile at that.

So whenever we play, each of us will try to remember this: I am a little Mary. Then our angels will never be ashamed of us. Slogan: *I am a little Mary.* (Consecration.)

*Third Talk*

(Review slogan.)

Do some children ever play where they should not play? (Comments.) (List places named. Try to include church, bus, class-time, etc.)

Now we all know why we should not play in those

places. (Comments.) But some children want to play all the time. They do not know when to stop. So, let us remember our slogan. That will help us.

I am sure each one of you loves Mother and Daddy. You don't want to worry them. The best way, then, is to play in safe places. And you will take care of little brother and sister, too, so they will be safe.

Let us see how many slogans we can say. (Have various children volunteer.) I wonder if we think of them at the right time. It is just like our conscience whispering to us. We listen and then we do the right thing. We act like Mary. And isn't she glad. She watches over her little Marys in a very special way. (Renew consecration.)

### Suggested Reading

"Revelations" Mary of Agreda: P. J. Kenedy, New York.

"The Secret of Mary" by St. Louis De Montfort, Montfort Publications, Bay Shore, N.Y. 11706.

CHAPTER VI

## MARY FULL OF GRACE

*First Talk*

(Picture of the Annunciation. Discuss the picture. Review the story.)

When you say the Rosary, what prayer do you say most? Who said that prayer first? I am sure all the angels wanted to take the message to Mary. But God sent Gabriel.

All heaven was looking down and listening that day. God, the Father, was listening. God, the Son, was listening. God, the Holy Ghost, was listening. And they were very pleased when Mary said, "Be it

**MARY FULL OF GRACE**

done as you say." Then Gabriel bowed before Mary and flew back to heaven with the news.

Can you guess why Mary was so pleasing to God? (Comments.) Yes, but what God liked most was this. Mary did not think much of herself. Many of the Jewish girls wished that some day they could be the Saviour's mother. But Mary never dreamed of such a thing. She thought it would be lovely to just baby-sit for the Holy Christ Child. And it would, wouldn't it?

But God picked Mary out for much more than just that. She was the only one God would choose. No one else was ever to be like her. And all the while she never thought much of herself.

Sometimes boys and girls think they are better than others. They are mean. They won't speak. Is that acting like Mary? I hope no one here acts like that. (Comments.)

Now whenever we say the Hail Mary let us remember something. Let us think why Mary was so pleasing to God. And if we want God to be pleased with us what shall we do? (Comments.) (Renew consecration.)

*Second Talk*

(Picture of the Visitation.)

When Gabriel left Mary what do you think she did? (Comments.) Well, Mary remembered that Gabriel had told her another happy secret. Her cousin Elizabeth was going to have a baby boy. And Mary knew how long Elizabeth had prayed for a baby. So Mary forgot all about herself. She said, "Elizabeth will need me. I must go to help her. I must go now."

Mary said, "Now." She didn't wait. Mary likes that word "now." So she went.

As soon as Elizabeth saw Mary she knew Mary's secret. And she said, "Blessed art thou among women." Wasn't that what Gabriel had said? I wonder how Elizabeth knew? Just think, she was the next one after Gabriel to say those holy words. I am sure that all the Elizabeths and Bettys are glad they have her name.

Well, Mary stayed with her cousin a while, and helped take care of little John. That was the baby's name.

Now when we say the Hail Mary we have many lovely things to think of. Of course, that prayer is longer now. And the last part asks Mary to do something. (Comments.) Yes, to pray for us when? Remember that little word? Mary likes to hear us say, "Now," so that we keep good. And she likes the other part. What is it? Yes, "at the hour of our death." Let us say it together. We do not know when that will be. But we know this. Mary will be praying for us then. Aren't we glad we belong to her? We will say our consecration with all our hearts.

*Third Talk*

This little talk tells us how Our Lady loves to hear the Hail Mary.

Once there was a little boy named Bernard. He lived in a big castle. Did you ever see a picture of a castle? Well, anyway, Bernard had good times after school playing with his brothers and his little sister.

But Bernard always found time in between to slip

away and pray. We could really call him Our Lady's Mario. You see he loved her so much.

When he grew up, guess what he did. (Comments.) Some of you have guessed right. He became a monk. (Explain.) Well, the monks were very holy. They made sacrifices every day. And they all had a special love for Mary.

Near the monks' chapel was a statue of the Blessed Mother. Every time Bernard passed it, he looked up and said, "Hail Mary." Now that happened very often. One day he was coming near the statue. He was thinking how lovely Mary must be. In a minute he was in front of her. He looked up and whispered, "Hail Mary." And right away he heard, "Hail Bernard." It came straight from the statue. Bernard was so happy he almost forgot where he was. He knew now how much Our Lady loved the words he had said. And was he glad he had said them so often? Then he made up his mind to do something. Can you tell? And maybe we could make up our minds to say them very, very often, too. Perhaps Our Lady answers us back when we say them, only we can't hear her. She let Bernard hear her that time because he was so holy. He really is one of Mary's very dear saints up in heaven.

So, what is it Mary listens for? Slogan: *Mary listens for the Hail Mary.* Suppose we say it now for all little Marys and Marios. (Renew consecration.)

*Fourth Talk*

What does Mary listen for? Would you like to hear a wonderful Hail Mary story?

This happened years ago. The Turks were very bad to the Catholics. Selim, their leader, made up his mind to fight them. And he was going to do as much damage as he could. A day was set for a terrible battle.

The Pope felt very bad about it all. So he called for men to fight. Hundreds of them, and even boys offered to help. And they said, "We don't want any pay. We are glad to fight for God and Our Lady." Even Prince John came from his beautiful palace and took charge of the ships.

On the morning of the battle the Prince and all his men went to Holy Communion. Then they sailed out to meet the Turks.

The Pope had begged all the priests and people to say the Rosary while the battle was going on. And then he told Our Lady, "Dear Lady of the Rosary, you must listen to all our Hail Marys. Please help the sailors. I will not eat or drink or sleep until you make us win." Then he began his long prayer. And of course all you could hear in churches and homes was the Rosary. Even the sailors on the ships were praying out loud.

Nearer and nearer came the Turks in their big ships. And so many you couldn't count them. The Christian navy was so small it made Selim laugh.

At last the fight began. Our sailors had to fight hard. They could not hold a Rosary in their hands. So what do you think they did? Each man hung his Rosary on his arm and kept right on fighting. Then all of a sudden one big Turkish ship went down. And then another. And it kept on like that. But not one Christian ship was sunk. And not one was damaged.

Suddenly the Turkish leader gave these orders, "Sail away fast! The Christians are helped by their God!" So the battle ended for the Christians. But on their way home, the Turks had a bad time of it. A terrible storm came up and sank every ship that was left. The Turks didn't dare come back any more.

Now, the Pope was in Rome far from the battle. But as soon as it stopped, he came out of his room. He held up his Rosary and said, "We have won the battle." I wonder how he knew. (Comments.) Yes, I suppose Our Lady told him. She did not want to keep him waiting.

That all happened on the first Sunday of October. So the Pope made that Sunday to be Rosary Sunday for always. He was Pope Pius V, the Pope of the Rosary. Think of all the Hail Marys that were said on that great day. And think of all the Hail Marys that are said when families say the Rosary. You see what a powerful prayer it is. See if we could make up a slogan about that. (Let the children give their suggestions.) (Renew consecration.)

### Suggested Reading

"Our Lady's Feasts" by Sister Mary Jean Dorsey; Sheed & Ward, New York.

"Mary's Garden of Roses" by Rev. Hugh Blunt: P. J. Kenedy, New York.

"Glories of Mary" by St. Alphonsus Liguori: Benziger Bros., New York.

"Ear of God" by Rev. Patrick Peyton: Doubleday, New York.

**MARY'S FIRST CHRISTMAS**

# CHAPTER VII

# MARY'S FIRST CHRISTMAS

*First Talk*

(Have the usual audio-visual aids for this story.)

Suppose all of us little Marys and Marios go on a journey. We shall go to Nazareth first. That is where the angel told Mary a wonderful secret. We shall listen to Saint Joseph, "Mary, we have to go to Bethlehem. The king says so." "Very well, Joseph," answers Mary, "if the king says so, we must go."

We wait quietly until Mary and Joseph are ready to go. They have just a little bundle of things and a donkey. Joseph helps Mary on to the donkey. And what does he do? Yes, and it will be a long, long walk.

At last they get to Bethlehem. Let us keep close to them. Joseph knocks at a door, and at another, and another. Each time he asks to go in for the night. But he always gets the same answer, "We have no room." Along comes a man and tells Joseph to go to a stable down the road. Joseph turns to Mary and says, "A stable, Mary, a stable." "Never mind, Joseph, it is all right," says Mary, "God will take care of us."

And down they go to the poor stable. There they find the ox and the ass just finishing their supper out of a manger. (Explain.) Mary kneels down on the straw, while Joseph tries to tidy the poor place. Then Joseph steps out to look at the stars. They are trying their best to make the sky beautiful tonight. Twinkle, twinkle, they seem to be whispering a secret to one another. When Joseph goes back into the stable, Mary is still kneeling. Her hands are folded. She is looking down. Joseph goes to look, too. And there on the straw lies Baby Jesus. Yes, here He is, all the way from heaven, just for us. Mary and Joseph cannot stop looking at the little Saviour.

Let us close our eyes and picture the Holy Child on the straw this first Christmas night. Now suppose you really had been there. What would you have done to help? (Comments.) Yes, and the lovely thing is this. When we help other poor children we help Jesus. He said so.

Wasn't that a lovely trip we took? (Comments.) When Christmas comes we can go and visit the Crib. And we will be sure to thank Jesus for coming. We will wish Him a Happy Birthday. Let us say our consecration to His wonderful Mother. She is our Mother, too.

## Second Talk

Remember the trip we took. Well, while we were peeping into the Stable something was going on near Bethlehem. Shepherds were minding their sheep. All of a sudden they saw the sky lighted up. In the light was an angel. At first the shepherds were scared. But the angel said, "Don't be afraid. I have good news for you. The Saviour is born. You will find Him in a manger in Bethlehem." Then crowds of angels came and sang a sweet Christmas song. When they finished they went back to heaven.

The shepherds looked at one another. And when they found that each one heard the same good news, they knew it was true. So over to Bethlehem they went. It was the happiest walk they ever had.

Now Joseph had just put clean straw into the manger. And Mary had laid her little Jesus in it. Joseph heard footsteps outside. He went to see who was there. Can you guess who it was? (Comments.) When they told Joseph about the angel, he let them all in.

Then Mary showed the shepherds the dear little Jesus. They fell on their knees and just looked and looked. Do you think Mary was glad that they came? (Comments.) Yes, she is always pleased when anyone visits Jesus, no matter who it is.

Where can we visit Jesus? (Comments.) Sometimes we are riding along in a car or train. We don't miss anything along the way. All of a sudden we see a church. We know this — the church has a Tabernacle. And Who is in the Tabernacle waiting there? Yes, and He is pleased when we remember Him. And how glad it makes Our Lady. She wants us to love our Lord so much. So now let us say our consecration to His dear Mother.

### Third Talk

Who came to see the little Lord in the manger? How did they know He was there? Well, later on some others came. They were the Three Wise Kings from far away.

A wonderful new star was in the sky. They said, "This must be the Saviour's Star. It means that He is born. We must go to see Him." You see they had learned about that from the Bible. So the Kings started off on their camels. And right away the Star moved ahead of them. All they had to do was follow. It took many days to ride over the desert. Does anyone know what a desert is? (Comments.) Well, at last they came to a big city, but the Star was gone.

So they went to King Herod and told him about the Star and everything. Now Herod got very excited. So he asked some smart men about the Star. They told him it was the Star of the Saviour. They told Herod He would be a king, and be born in Bethlehem. Herod did not like that at all, but he did not let on. He just said to the Wise Men, "You go and find where this little King is. Then come back and tell me. I want to visit Him, too." So the Wise Men promised.

As soon as they started off, the wonderful Star came back. It moved before them until it came to the place where Jesus was. Then it stood still. Joseph heard the jingle of bells. He peeped out. And there were the Kings jumping off their camels. In a minute they saw the little King resting in the Queen's arms. Who was the Queen? (Comments.) She let them stay as long as they wanted. It was like Christmas night. Then the kings gave gifts to Mary for their little King. Each gift was something they liked very much. They wanted to make a sacrifice. Wasn't that lovely? And we shall do the same when we say our consecration.

*Fourth Talk*

What did you like best in the Christmas story? (Comments.)

Christmas will soon be here. We must be getting many gifts ready for the Holy Child. And of course we shall offer them through the hands of Mary. Isn't that what the Kings did?

When we visit the Crib we can ask little Jesus — how did You like the toys I gave up for the poor, or the way I helped at home, or the way I tried in school? We won't hear Jesus' answer but we can guess what it will be. He knows we give all to His Mother. And she makes everything we do look better.

When we look at the tiny Baby lying in the manger, we remember that He is God. And we can remember something else when we go to Holy Communion. Each of our hearts will be a little manger, only much nicer. The manger could not love Him. But our hearts can.

Isn't God good to us? How much we should love Him. How can we show that we love Him? (Comments.) Yes, and keeping close to Mary will help. Slogan: *Keep close to Mary*. So let us say our consecration.

*Suggested Reading*

"Jesus, Son of Mary" by Most Rev. Fulton J. Sheen: Declan McMullen Co., New York.

"Story of Jesus" by Catherine Beebe: Bruce Pub. Co., Milwaukee, Wis.

"The Christ Child" by Maude and Miska Petersham: Doubleday, New York.

"A Life of Jesus for Children" by Marigold Hunt: Sheed & Ward, New York.

**MARY AND HER MEDAL**

# CHAPTER VIII

# MARY'S MEDAL

*First Talk*

Would you like to hear a story about a little Mary? This little Mary lived many, many years ago. Her name was Zoe. Zoe had some big brothers and a couple of little sisters. So you can see she was just in between.

When the boys wanted a job done they usually ran to Zoe. And when the little ones were getting in mother's way, big sister was sure to be there to play with them and tell them stories. She was the darling of the family.

One day the busy mother caught a very bad cold. She got worse and worse. In a few days she went to heaven. The whole family was very sad. For days and days poor Zoe could not stop crying.

One evening she finished her lessons and began to tidy up the living room. As she looked up at the statue of Our Lady she got a happy idea. She took the statue in her arms and cuddled it close to her heart. She begged the Blessed Virgin to be her mother. And from that time on Zoe was sure that Mary was truly her mother in a very special way. There was no more crying after that. And very soon she began to make her father and the others happy again. How do you think she did it? (Comments.) (Consecration.)

*Second Talk*

Here is another story about Zoe. We know she loved Our Lady. Well, every night before going to sleep she asked her angel to let her see the Blessed

Virgin. Just think of that! All of us will be sure to look for God's dear Mother as soon as we get into heaven, but Zoe didn't want to wait until then.

After Zoe grew up she went away to be a Sister. Her name was Sister Catherine. And every night she still kept asking her angel to let her see her Blessed Mother.

One night, Sister Catherine was sound asleep. All of a sudden she heard someone call, "Catherine, come." She woke up and heard it again. Then she rubbed her eyes and looked around. There beside her bed stood a beautiful child. It was her angel. He was beckoning her to come, and he said, "Our Lady is waiting for you. Follow me." You can imagine how surprised Sister Catherine felt — and how happy.

She dressed quickly and followed her good angel. All the lights went on and the doors of the chapel opened by themselves. Sister Catherine thought she was in a dream but she kept right on after the angel. Straight into the chapel, and up into the Sanctuary they went.

In a minute the happy little Sister saw Our Lady. She was, oh, so beautiful! She sat down on a chair and called Sister Catherine to her. And guess what? Sister knelt down and put her hands on Mary's lap. Then they had a long, happy talk together. When the Blessed Virgin had finished, she went back to heaven. But Sister Catherine kept looking at the empty chair.

The angel touched Sister Catherine and she knew she must go back to bed. As they left the chapel the door closed and the lights went out.

When Sister reached her room, the angel disappeared. But there was no more sleep for Sister that night. Why? (Comments.) (Consecration.)

*Third Talk*

(Review the story of the apparition. Have a miraculous medal to show the children.)

Sister Catherine never forgot Our Lady's visit. Many times she thanked her for coming. One day while Sister was in the chapel, Mary came again. She told Sister that she wanted her to have a medal made. And she said, "It is to be like this." Mary stood with her hands reaching down. On her fingers were beautiful jewels. These jewels sent out rays of light, shining down over the whole world. There was an oval frame around Mary. (Draw it on the blackboard.) It was made of gold letters. The holy words said, "O Mary conceived without sin, pray for us who have recourse to thee." Slowly the medal turned around. On the back was a cross over the letter M (draw it) and two hearts—the hearts of Jesus and Mary.

Mary told Sister Catherine that the medal was to be blessed and worn around the neck. She promised, "Those who wear it shall receive great graces." The rays of light coming from Mary's hands were graces for all of us. And the more we ask for, the more we shall get. Now think of that! Isn't it wonderful?

After a long time the medals were made. So many graces and blessings came to those who wore a medal, that it is called the Miraculous Medal. (Show the medal to the children. Urge them to wear it, or better still, have them enrolled, if possible.)

Wasn't it lovely of Our Lady to give us her medal? How happy we should be that we belong to her.

Let us say our consecration today to give special thanks to our Blessed Mother. (Post for memorization the ejaculation and Mary's promise. Explain the meaning of the ejaculation.)

*Fourth Talk*

Here is a Medal story.

Joey had lived with the Sisters for a long time. He was only two when his new mother took him. He did not say a word, but just gave her a happy smile.

On their way out they passed a statue of Our Lady. The baby boy pointed to it and said, "Mary." That was the first word he had spoken to his new mother. It made her so happy because she loved Our Lady. And she made up her mind that little Joey would grow up a real Mario.

When Joey was nearly three he got very sick. Doctors at the hospital said that if he did get better he would be blind and crippled. The sickness was almost as bad as Polio. One doctor told his mother to pray that Joey would die.

But Joey's mother said, "Mary will help." So she took her boy home and put the Miraculous Medal on him. Then she began to wheel him to the novena in a baby carriage. You see his legs were crippled.

Mother and Dad prayed for some weeks. They noticed that Joey's eyes were getting better. He never missed a thing. The pains were better, too. And he began to crawl around pretty lively. You can guess the rest. (Comments.) Yes, and our Joey was quick as a squirrel.

Joey's mother is still thanking Our Lady, and getting lots of people to wear the medal.

And Joey—well, he is a fine, tall lad. He can go quicker than a squirrel now, because he is in the Air Force. He has wings! (Comments.)

(Ejaculation. Renew consecration.)

### Suggested Reading

"The Medal" by Mary F. Windeatt: Grail Publications, St. Meinrad, Indiana.

"She Kept the Secret of Her Queen" by Rev. J. Husslein: Bruce Pub. Co., Milwaukee, Wis.

"Song of the Dove" by Mary F. Todd: P. J. Kenedy, New York.

"Little Catherine of the Miraculous Medal" by A Daughter of Charity: Benziger Bros., New York.

CHAPTER IX

## MARY'S ROSARY

*First Talk*

Dominic had always been Our Lady's little Mario. His dear mother had taught him how. All his life he had asked Mary to help him, and she did. And at last he was what he always wanted to be—a priest.

Now it happened that many, many people were heretics. That meant that they did not believe all the things about God that you and I believe. They would believe only what they liked, and no one could change their minds at all, not even priests.

Dominic felt bad about all this. So he made up his mind that he would make these heretics give up their bad ideas about things. He talked to them, and

**MARY'S ROSARY**

he prayed to Our Lady. Nothing happened. Instead, they began to be nasty to Dominic. They made fun of him and threw things at him.

One day he was going along a lonely road. Suddenly, he saw some heretics coming toward him. They made faces at him and shook their fists. Dominic thought they were going to beat him up. The men ran up to him and waved clubs in the air. "We have you now," said the leader.

But Dominic was not even a little bit afraid. "What do you want me for?" he asked.

"We want to kill you," shouted one.

"Well, what are you waiting for?" said the priest. "Go ahead."

But somehow or other they did not go ahead. The leader said, "You don't seem scared of us."

"Why should I be," said the priest. "If you kill me I shall go to heaven sooner."

Dominic stared right at them. And would you believe it, one by one they put down their clubs. The priest's face was so holy they were frightened to death. Before you could count three, they turned and ran off. Dominic looked after them and chuckled. All he could see was heels. Then he folded his hands and thanked Someone. (Comments.)

Mary always helps, doesn't she? Let us remember that.

Slogan: *Mary always helps.* (Renew consecration.)

*Second Talk*
One day Dominic thought he would try some-

thing new with his heretics. He got a large sheet of paper. On it he wrote a long list of questions about the things they believed. He sent the paper to the leader. And he invited him to come and have a friendly talk about these questions. Dominic was hoping that he could make this heretic see his awful mistake.

When the time came for the meeting, it was very chilly. Dominic lighted a fire in the yard next to the church. That was where they were to talk things over.

Along came the leader and his crowd. They looked at the fire, whispered, and poked one another. Then they laughed and nodded to the leader.

"Father Dominic," said the leader, "we won't bother talking about the questions. We have a better plan."

"What is your plan?" asked Dominic.

"Well," said the man, "I'll put your paper in the fire. If it burns, you are wrong and we are right."

"All right," said Dominic quietly, and he kept on praying.

So down went the paper into the middle of the fire. The smart heretics began to jump around and clap their hands. But they clapped too soon. Flames curled all around the paper, but that was all. In a few minutes, up it came. It took off like a little airplane, and away it flew over their heads. Then it dipped and landed at Dominic's feet. He smiled and picked it up. It wasn't even scorched. The heretics were so mad they just walked off shaking their fists.

Why didn't the paper burn? (Comments.)

Who helped Dominic? Yes, *Mary always helps*. (Renew consecration.)

*Third Talk*

Dominic had a hard time of it, didn't he? Do you think he gave up? No, indeed!

One day he began to tell Mary how much he had prayed for these foolish people. "Dear Mother," he said, "when are you going to help these poor sinners?"

"Right now," answered a beautiful voice. It was the voice that sang little Jesus to sleep. And there was Mary telling him what she would do. It was just lovely. She gave Dominic the Rosary and told him to teach it to priests and people. It was to be Our Lady's own way of getting the heretics back to God, her Son. Dominic thanked Mary for her goodness. She smiled at him and disappeared.

In no time at all priests and people were saying the Rosary. Then the heretics began one by one to slip into the back of the church. This time they came to listen to the priests. Very soon they were praying the Rosary, too. After a little while hundreds were doing the same. At last the power of the Rosary smashed the bad ideas of the heretics. And wasn't that just what Mary wanted? (Comments.)

So that is the story of how the Rosary began. And how glad Our Lady must be that so many of you love it and say it. (Comments.)

Dominic became a great saint. You see all the saints loved Our Lady, and so St. Dominic happens to be one of her special saints.

Let us keep close to Our Lady and try to copy her all we can.

(Renew consecration.)

*Fourth Talk*

What was our last slogan? And whom did Mary help? (Comments.)

Mary's lovely Rosary helps all kinds of people. Our new story tells how she helped a circus girl.

This girl had swung from the trapeze so often that it was just play for her. Well, one night she started out, but something went wrong. And down she fell. The poor girl was badly hurt. Doctors said she would not get better.

She lay on her bed terribly sick and frightened. One of the nurses called the priest. You know there is always a priest handy in the hospital.

The priest came and asked her if she would like to go to Confession. But the girl shook her head and said, "No, Father, there is no use. I am too bad. God will not forgive me."

Father talked kindly to her and said, "Just as soon as you are sorry and say 'O my God, I am heartily sorry,' God is ready to take away all your sins."

After a few minutes the girl made her Confession. Then Father anointed her (simple explanation) and brought her Holy Communion.

Next morning Father slipped in to see her. She looked bad but she was very happy. Then Father said to her, "You could have died right away when you fell. But God gave you a chance to make up with Him. Now you are ready for heaven. What good thing did you do to get such a blessing as this?"

The girl answered, "Father, I never did anything good. But I did say a Rosary every night."

"Ah, that's it," said the priest, "and Mary did not forget you."

"No," said the girl, "and here she is!" And with a happy smile, she died. Mary had come to take her to heaven.

What do you think of the Rosary now? (Comments.)

(Renew consecration.)

### Suggested Reading

"St. Dominic" by Joan Windham: Sheed & Ward, New York.

"St. Dominic and the Rosary" by Catherine Beebe: Farrar, Straus & Cudahy, New York.

"Pray the Rosary Daily" (Illustrated, full color leaflet): Montfort Publications, Bay Shore, N.Y.

"The Secret of the Rosary" by St. Louis De Montfort: Montfort Publications, Bay Shore, N.Y. 11706.

CHAPTER X

# MARY'S MESSAGE

*First Talk*

What was our last slogan? Yes, and Mary will keep on helping us if we keep on asking.

A long time ago Our Lady wanted to tell the world something important. So one day in springtime she looked down and saw three children tending their sheep. She saw them sit down to eat their lunch. She saw them say their Rosary, too. And right after this she saw them get ready to play.

So Mary said, "I will tell these children what I want. They love me, and they will do whatever I ask them."

**MARY'S MESSAGE**

In a few minutes the children saw a flash of lightning, and then another. Lucy, who was ten, began to run and so did her two cousins. Just as they got to a small tree, they saw a beautiful sight. There above the tree was a lovely Lady. She was all shining like light. A golden Rosary hung from her hands. Then Lucy heard her sweet voice.

"Do not be afraid. I will not hurt you."

"Where do you come from, and what do you want of me?" asked Lucy.

"I am from heaven. I want you to come here again. Then I will tell you more."

Lucy asked Our Lady if she and her cousins would go to heaven. Our Lady said they would but that Francis would have to say many Rosaries. Sometimes he liked to hurry up with his prayers and go to play.

Before our dear Lady left, she asked her little ones for sacrifices. And right away Lucy said, "Yes, yes!" Mary smiled and went slowly up to heaven. The children kept looking until she was out of sight. Then they had to go home with the sheep.

Lucy did not want anyone to know about the Lady. But Jacinta forgot and told — she was only six. In no time, everyone knew the story.

The two mothers were very cross. They did not believe a word of it. Lucy was punished many times. All the neighbors were making fun of her and of her cousins. But when the children thought of the lovely Lady, they could accept everything for her.

"We can offer it up for sinners," said Francis. "That's what the Lady asked us to do."

Now wasn't that fine for a boy of eight? He was learning to be a real Mario, wasn't he?

I wonder if we would do something like that. And how many would have said, "Yes, yes!" to Our Lady.

Slogan: We will say, *"Yes, yes!" to our dear Lady.* (Renew consecration.)

## Second Talk

Do you remember what Our Lady promised the children? And what is our slogan?

What was the last thing Our Lady asked the children to do?

Yes, and they were counting the days for Mary's next visit. It came at last. So the children went to the Cova. That was the name of the place.

They had just begun the Rosary when Lucy called out, "Here she comes." She was so bright and beautiful that they could hardly look at her.

Our Lady told them to keep on saying the Rosary every day. And then a strange thing happened. The ground seemed to open, and they looked into a big fire. It was terrible to see souls in the flames. But in a few minutes it was all over.

Our Lady said, "You have seen hell, where souls go who die in mortal sin. I want you to make little sacrifices so that sinners may be saved from going there."

Lucy and her cousins could never forget that dreadful sight. Jacinta said that, if people only knew how terrible it was, they would run away from sin.

You know God does not want anyone to go to hell. Neither does Our Lady. Souls go there for mortal sins. That means big sins they do on purpose, and don't care about. All they would have to do is tell God they are sorry. Of course, they must mean what they say and go to Confession.

Our dear Lady had another important thing to tell. She said that if people would keep the Commandments and pray the Rosary every day, something fine would happen. Russia would turn to God.

Then Mary left her dear little children and went back to heaven. The little ones watched her until she was out of sight. I am sure they wanted to follow her. (Comments.)

Now I think many little Marys and Marios are trying to do what Our Lady wants. She asks only for little sacrifices. And we can do so many of them every day. (Comments.) And when we give them into her hands, we know what will happen. All will please her holy heart. We call it her Immaculate Heart, because it never had a single sin. (Renew consecration.)

*Third Talk*

I suppose you think that Lucy and her cousins were having a happy time. No indeed! Lucy was treated very badly at home. And people were still laughing at each of them.

Besides, Our Lady had told them a secret. Nearly everyone was asking them to tell the secret. But they would not tell it. Even the Mayor wanted the secret. So he took them to jail and said he would fry them in a pan. Do you think they told him? (Comments.) Not at all! Francis and Jacinta said, "We won't tell. If he kills us it will be a big sacrifice. And we will go to heaven." Weren't they brave! (Comments.) So they didn't tell a word of the secret. Anyway the Mayor did not fry them. He let them go. And very soon they saw the heavenly Lady. She made them so happy they forgot about the wicked Mayor.

Mary smiled at her dear children. She was pleased with them. They were doing lots of hard things, even sharing their lunch with other poor children.

Lucy asked Our Lady if she and her cousins were going to heaven soon. Our Lady said, "Francis and Jacinta will come very soon. But you will have to wait a long, long time. You must tell people about me. You must tell them how to love my Immaculate Heart. And the next time I come, I shall work a miracle. Then people will believe you."

Lucy was glad about the miracle. But she felt very sad about staying on earth so long. Her cousins told her that she was doing the hardest sacrifice of all. Then Lucy felt better. These children really loved Our Lady. Can you tell me why? (Comments.)

Let us say some of our slogans. They will help us to love her and copy her. (Consecration.)


*Fourth Talk*

At last the day came for the miracle that Our Lady promised. And you can be sure that more crowds came for that. It had poured rain all night and morning. But Fatima (that was the name of the place) was packed just the same. Everybody was soaked, and still they waited.

All of a sudden Our Lady came. The people could see and hear Lucy talking to her. But they could not see or hear the heavenly Lady. Lucy asked Our Lady if she wanted anything else. Mary answered that she wanted a church there. And she told Lucy this, "I am the Lady of the Rosary."

By that time the rain had stopped and the sky was clear. And then the miracle happened. The sun came out and began to spin around like a pin-wheel. All the colors of the rainbow were coming from it. People, trees, and ground were all colors. How do you think the people felt? (Comments.) Well, they were terribly scared. Some thought it was the end of the world. At last the sun stopped spinning and went back to its place.

Then another wonderful thing happened. When the people looked down at their clothes, they were all dry. You would think it hadn't rained at all. That's how Our Lady took care of the people. They had come so far and waited so long. There was no more laughing at the little shepherds. People believed them now.

While the sun was spinning around, St. Joseph came with little Jesus. And little Jesus blessed the people. The children said that the Child Jesus was very beautiful.

And so Our Lady went back to heaven. She had come to the children six times. This was her last visit to the Cova at Fatima.

What did Our Lady ask for each time she came? (Comments.) Yes, and it makes her very happy to see so many little Marys and Marios doing these things.

What do you think of the Rosary now? (Comments.) Yes, and that is why she gave it to St. Dominic. As long as we live, we shall say our Rosary. Let us whisper that to Our Lady.

(Renew consecration.)

### Suggested Reading

"Our Lady Came to Fatima" by R. F. Hume: Farrar, Straus, & Cudahy, New York.

"Our Lady of Fatima" by Wm. T. Walsh: Macmillan Co., New York.

"Children of Fatima" by Mary F. Windeatt: Grail Publications, St. Meinrad, Indiana.

"Jacinta, the Flower of Fatima" by Joseph Galamba de Oliviera: Catholic Book Pub. Co., New York.

CHAPTER XI

## MARY'S ALTAR BOY

*First Talk*

Do you ever go about in your bare feet? Here's a boy who did. You see his mother and father were poor. And shoes cost a lot. So he wore them only to church. In the fields he wore wooden clogs when he helped his father.

I suppose you want to know this boy's name. Well, it was Beppo. Sounds funny, doesn't it? And Beppo was just full of fun.

His mother prayed to Our Lady for a little boy. When he was only one day old, he was christened Joseph. But she always called him Beppo.

Beppo loved the Blessed Mother. He wanted to be her altar boy. At last he was, and a real Mario, too.

Can you tell why? Yes, and besides, he tried to make everyone happy. When his good mother looked worried he had funny stories to make her smile. No wonder she loved him so much.

The boys in the neighborhood liked Beppo, too. He was the leader in all games. But when Beppo went to the sacristy to get ready for the altar, that was different. The other altar boys tried to make him laugh. Beppo got dressed and paid no attention. He was like an angel in church.

How do you think Our Lady felt when she saw her Beppo on the altar? (Comments.) I hope she feels that way when she sees us in church. (Renew consecration.)

*Second Talk*

Who remembers the last thing we said about Our Lady's altar boy? Yes, and can you guess what he was always wishing for? Janie guessed it—his First Communion. He had to wait until he was eleven. So when that day came you can imagine how happy Beppo was. It was the happiest he had been yet. On that day he whispered a secret to our Lord. The secret was this: He wanted to be a priest.

Beppo knew he would have to study many years. He would need money and his family was poor. He talked it over with his mother. This good mother said, "Don't be sad, Beppo. We shall say our Rosary for this every evening. Our Lady will help you." Beppo was glad that he always led the Rosary after the dishes were washed.

**MARY'S ALTAR BOY**

Remember our slogan: Mary always _____. She helped here, too. A priest got Beppo into high school. This school was far away. And he would have to walk. He did not mind that. But he needed shoes to wear in school. Where would he get them? Well, his dear mother used some money she had been saving and bought him a pair.

One fine morning Beppo started off to his new school. Now what do you think he did with his new shoes? No, he slung them over his shoulders and walked the long, long road barefoot. When he got near school he put his shoes on. Can you guess why he carried his shoes every day instead of wearing them? (Comments.) He had to be saving, didn't he?

Well, Beppo studied for years. He was always first in class. And all the while he was loving God and Our Lady more and more. He knew that he must keep close to Mary because Mary gets us all the graces we need.

Then at last the great day came when he was made a priest. That day was the happiest of his life. And we must call him Father Sarto, for that was his name.

What do you like best in this story? (Comments.) And what slogan could we make? This will help. Mary gets us _____. (Renew consecration.)

*Third Talk*
(Suitable pictures.)

Father Sarto was very good to the poor. He loved boys and girls. And many a game he played with them. He told them stories about Our Lady. Everyone loved him. And they were happy when he was made a Cardinal.

Many years later the Pope died. Now there must be a new one. And who do you think was made Pope? Yes, Cardinal Sarto had been so kind and so holy that they said he was just the one.

But Cardinal Sarto didn't think so. "No, no," he said, "I can never be the Pope." But all the other Cardinals said, "Our Lady will help you." And right away the new Pope said, "All right, I will be Pope Pius X."

Pope Pius had always felt sorry that children had to wait so long for First Communion. So he said, "Now that I am Pope I must do something about this. Our dear Lord loved to have the children near Him. When the Apostles wanted to chase them away, He would not let them. He wanted the children to come to Him. And I am sure He wants them now. If little ones went to Bethlehem, Our Lady let them come in. She let them take Jesus' little Hand. And maybe she let them hold Him. Surely Mary is glad now when little ones have Jesus in their hearts."

So the Holy Father gave orders that even first and second graders should have Holy Communion. Wasn't Pope Pius kind? Of course, he said that they must get their hearts ready. They must try to be better, pray, and make little sacrifices.

Now isn't that what we little Marys and Marios are doing in this class? And Mary is watching every day. Then when the great day comes she will get us many graces. (Comments.) (Renew consecration.)

*Fourth Talk*

(Suitable pictures.)

What did Pius X do for God's little ones?

One day he was thanking our Lord for letting him do it. Then he began to think of all the little children that would ever make their First Holy Communion. All God's dear children—Chinese, Japanese, Indians, Eskimos. And he knew our Lord wanted just that. And he knew someone else wanted it. (Comments.)

Yes, indeed! Mary would see all her dear boys and girls kneeling at the altar rail. They would have Jesus in their hearts. And how much they would love Him. The same Jesus that Mary laid in the _____ (let children supply). The same Jesus that lived with her and St. Joseph at _____. The same kind Jesus Who blessed little _____. Good Jesus, Who was nailed to the _____. Dear Jesus Who died for _____.

So the Holy Father was very happy about it. Then he said, "From now on big people and children can go to Communion often. They can go every day if they are ready. Then every day will be like Christmas." Why?

This holy Father was once little Beppo. Remember how he carried his shoes on his back? Remember how he loved Our Lady? Well, he now he is Saint Pius X. He is one of Mary's special saints. Let us make our consecration. Perhaps St. Pius will listen while we say it. Then we can say another prayer. St. Pius, pray for us now and on our First Communion Day.

*Suggested Reading*

"The Burning Flame" by F. B. Thornton: Benziger Bros., New York.

"The Children's Pope" by Teri Martini: Catechetical Guild, St. Paul, Minn.

"The White Knight" by Mabel Farnum: Catholic Library Service, St. Paul, Minn.

"The Great Mantle" by Katherine Burton: Longmans, Green & Co., New York.

CHAPTER XII

# MARY'S SMILE

*First Talk*

(Pictures of St. Therese as a child.)

Today's story is about a little girl named Therese. When Therese was very tiny her mother told her about Little Jesus and the Blessed Mother.

Therese loved to hear about them. She said, "I love Baby Jesus and His Mother." Her mother smiled and said, "Do you want to keep close to them?" "Oh, yes," said Therese. "Then you must always say 'yes' to them. You must do what they want," said her mother.

Well, Therese did just that. As she grew up, she always listened to the voice. And right away she did the better thing. And that was the same as saying yes to Jesus and Mary. Do you think Therese was a little Mary? (Comments.) Yes, she acted like Mary. Didn't Mary always say yes to God?

So now, if we want to act like Mary, we shall listen to the voice. Remember about the voice? It tells us when a thing is right and when a thing is wrong. Who knows the big name of it? If we listen and say yes, guess what? That will be a good way to get ready for our big day. And I think our guardian angels will be counting the days until First Communion.

Then let us keep on saying yes to God. And let us

**MARY'S SMILE**

copy His Mother. She's watching to see how we are getting ready. Let us give her some lovely surprises. Shall we? Slogan—*Always say yes to God.* (Consecration.)

## Second Talk

What was our last slogan? Who did that? So we know she was a real little Mary. She loved Our Lady with all her heart. Well, this story shows how much Mary loved Therese.

Therese had a dear kind mother. But the dear mother died. Her little girl cried and cried. Nothing could make her happy. Her father said, "Come, little Queen (he always called her that)—Mother is in heaven. She will never be sick again. She loves you up there just the same. And we all love you, too."

But Therese just shook her sad little head. In a few days, she was very sick. Indeed they were afraid she, too, would fly away to heaven. The doctor said that it would be a long time before Therese would be well again.

One day the dear child was very, very sick. Her sisters were kneeling around her bed. They were praying to Our Lady for help. Near the bed was a statue of our Blessed Mother. Therese loved to look at it. While they were praying, Our Lady turned her eyes toward Therese. She smiled at her darling little girl. Therese sat up and smiled back. And that very day she began to get better. When the doctor came the next day, Therese was singing. He opened his eyes wide. Therese gave him a big smile. She said, "I'm all right."

Wasn't Our Lady good to Therese? And she will be especially good to us, too. She will help us get our hearts ready for Holy Communion. I really think she will smile at us, too, on the great day. (Comments.) (Consecration.)

*Third Talk*

(Picture of Therese as First Communicant.)

What did Our Lady do for Therese? Now we shall see how Therese got ready for her First Communion. Her big sister, Pauline, had gone away to be a Sister. So her sister Marie helped Therese get her heart ready for little Jesus.

Marie taught Therese how to make flowers in her heart to please Jesus. Not flowers that we can see, but heavenly (spiritual) flowers. God could see them. All the good deeds and sacrifices would be so many flowers. Marie told Therese to give them to Mary. And we all know what Mary does with them.

Well, the great day came at last for Jesus and Therese. She had her dear Lord in her heart. Therese closed her eyes and talked to Him. She told Him how long she had been waiting for Him. She offered Him the flowers. And I wonder what else she could have told Him? (Comments. Let the children express their ideas freely.) Guess what she asked after that? She asked Him to let her be a Sister.

On that day Therese and all the other children in her class were consecrated to Our Lady. And Therese was chosen to say the consecration. She made the same consecration we make. She was another little Mary.

That same evening Therese had a pleasant time at home. Her father gave his little queen a beautiful watch. She told her sister Pauline she was happy about the nice time and the watch. Then she said this. The best gift of all was _____. She could not forget IT.

Very soon our happy day will be here. We, too, shall receive the best Gift that God can give us. And won't Our Lady be happy on that day? So do not forget the surprises. (Consecration.)

*Fourth Talk*

(Picture of St. Therese as a nun.)

What did Therese want to be? Yes, and she did not forget about it. When she grew up, she left her dear father. She left her sisters and her happy home. Therese made all these sacrifices for God. That is what all Sisters have done.

Anyway she was named Sister Therese of the Child Jesus. She worked a lot. She prayed a lot. And best of all, she loved Jesus and Mary a lot.

While Sister Therese swept or scrubbed, she was singing in her heart. She was always making lovely little verses about the good God and His sweet Mother.

But Sister Therese did not live long. Our Lord wanted her in heaven. So she got sick. And then one day, while she was saying, "My God I love You," her soul flew away to Jesus and Mary. From now on we shall call her Saint Therese. (Show picture.)

Therese is a saint because she said yes to God. She began when she was little, and she kept right on. Besides, she loved Our Lady.

What did you like best in this story? How many would like to make the heavenly flowers like St. Therese? Very well. When we tell the truth we make a lily. When we obey right away we make a violet. And each time we are nice to others we make a lovely rose. (Have some type of device as a reminder.) Shall we start today? These flowers will be more surprises.

Your happiest day is coming fast. I know you are going to please the Immaculate Heart of Mary. And our Lord will be glad to come to you because you are so close to her. And if any one of you wants to be a Sister or a priest, be sure to ask our Lord on that wonderful day. Now let's make our consecration better than ever.

### Suggested Reading

"Little Saint Therese" by Elizabeth von Schmidt-Pauli: Macmillan Co., New York.

"Her Little Way" by J. Clarke: Benziger Bros., New York.

"My Name Is Written in Heaven" by Frances P. Keyes: Julian Messner, New York.

"Sunshine and Saints" by D. H. Mosely: P. J. Kenedy, New York.

CHAPTER XIII

## MARY'S ROSES

*First Talk*

This story happened a good many years ago. It happened down in Mexico. That's the country right below us. It happened to a poor Indian. He had been baptized John only a few years before.

Well, one Saturday morning John was on his way to Mass. You know, Saturday is always Our Lady's

**MARY AND THE ROSES**

day. And John loved her dearly. So that is why he was going to Mass on Saturday.

As he was crossing Tepeyac Hill, he heard most beautiful music. It seemed like the singing of many birds. But there were no birds. It was winter time. Then the sweetest voice he ever heard, called "Dear John." He looked around and whom did he see but a lovely Lady. She was dressed like an Indian princess. A golden light was all around her. Everything on the old stony hill looked like gold.

She spoke again, "My son, where are you going?" John told her, "I am going to Mass in honor of God's Mother." When she heard that, her smile was beautiful. She answered, "John, I am the Mother of the true God. I am a merciful Mother. I listen to all prayers. I wish a church built right here. Go to the Bishop and tell him." And with that she was gone.

It was a long way to the Bishop. But John was so happy to do an errand for God's Mother, he forgot everything else. The Bishop did not believe him. He thought John was dreaming or something like that. The walk back was a sad one for poor John.

As he got near the hill he saw the golden light over everything. And there was our sweet Mother coming toward him. John fell on his knees. He told Our Lady that the Bishop did not believe him. He begged her to send someone else, someone better. But Our Lady did not seem to mind at all. She only smiled and said, "Listen, my dear son, I want you to do this. No one else will do. Go back to the Bishop tomorrow and tell him all over again."

Next morning, John went again. The Bishop listened. Then he told John to ask the Lady for a sign so that he could believe.

John was not so sad this time. He was sure Our Lady would give the sign. As he reached Tepeyac he saw the light. And again Mary was coming to meet him. He knelt down and gave her the Bishop's message. She was pleased, and said, "Yes, come here tomorrow. I shall give you the sign."

Do you like this poor Indian? (Comments.) Can you remember some of the things Mary told him about herself? (Comments.) Suppose we write them on the chalkboard. Could we make slogans out of them? Help the children to develop: *Mary is a merciful Mother. Mary listens to all prayers.* Surely all her little Marys and Marios are glad to remember these words. Let us make our consecration. We know she will be listening.

## Second Talk

Where did we leave John in our last story? Well, he almost ran home the rest of the way. (Comments.) But when he got there he found his uncle very sick. The poor old man was so bad that John could not leave him. There was no one else to stay with him. So John did not go for the sign the next day. The morning after that he rushed off to get the priest. His uncle was dying.

John took a short cut around Tepeyac this time. And what do you think? (Comments.) Yes, Our Lady took a short cut, too. There she stood smiling. The golden glow was all around her. Poor John begged her to let him go for the priest. He cried, "My uncle is dying."

"My dear son," said Mary. "Do not worry about your uncle. I have prayed for him. He is cured. Now go up to the rocks. Gather the roses you will find there. Bring them to me. I will wait here." John knew very well that roses do not grow on stones. And besides, wasn't it winter? But he did not say what he thought! He did what he was told. And what a surprise he got! Such a gorgeous sight! Lovely roses, and ah, so many! He could not count them. Well, he gathered as many as he could and put them in his tilma.

I don't suppose you ever heard of a tilma. Well, if you had a very long apron tied around your neck, that would be something like a tilma. But poor John's tilmas was not a bit pretty. It was made of very rough goods, something like a potato bag.

The precious roses were filling the air with a wonderful perfume. John hurried down the hill to Our Lady. He knelt down before her. She looked at the roses. Then with her own blessed fingers she placed each rose the way she wanted it. And John watched her touching his poor tilma.

"My son," she said, "take these to the Bishop. Do not show them to anyone else. These roses are the sign." And with a heavenly smile on her face she left him.

Isn't that a lovely story? (Comments.) I wonder why Our Lady loved John so much? (Comments.) Yes, she is pleased when we do what we are told right

off. Who would like to read the slogans? We can say
our consecration better now.

*Third Talk*
   (Picture of Our Lady at Guadalupe.)
   Do you still remember the rose story? Well, this
one is even lovelier. John started off for the Bishop's
house. He had to be careful of his precious bundle.
He was worried, too, about the servant. Each time he
went to see the Bishop they had made fun of him.
You see, he was only a poor Indian. It was the same
story this morning. They wanted to pull the tilma to
see what he was hiding. Then somehow or other, he
got in and met the Bishop. "Here is the sign," said
John. And he opened the tilma. All the lovely roses
tumbled over the floor. The whole place was filled
with the perfume. A crowd of servants came running
to the spot.
   John was still holding the tilma open. He won-
dered why the Bishop and the others were on their
knees. They were not even looking at Our Lady's
beautiful roses. They were staring at him. Some had
tears in their eyes. Some were praying out loud. John
looked down at his tilma. He could hardly believe his
eyes. It was no longer the poor old thing it had been.
Now he knew why they were looking. For there on his
tilma was a beautiful picture of God's Mother. It was
just as she looked at Tepeyac Hill. She was like an Indian princess. Her dress was rose-colored. Over her
head and down to her feet hung a beautiful green
cloak. It was sprinkled with stars.

The Bishop untied John's tilma and held it up before the people. And from that day to this the people of Mexico have Our Lady's picture. It has never faded. And no artist has even been able to paint one like it. (Show the picture.)

I suppose you think this the best story of all. (Comments.) What if you had been there when John opened his tilma? What do you think you would have said to Our Lady? (Comments.) Let us say our consecration with all our hearts.

*Fourth Talk*

(Show the picture. Let the children talk.)

When John got home he had lots to tell his uncle. And the uncle had lots to tell him. He gave John a big surprise.

"John," he said, "you don't have to tell me anything. Our Lady came to me. First she made me well. Then she told me about the picture on your tilma. She said that it was a sign for the Bishop. She wants her name to be Holy Mary of Guadalupe."

"Guadalupe?" said John. "I wonder why? There is no place around here called Guadalupe." "Well, that's what our dear Mother said," answered the uncle. "It's her secret."

And now the whole place has that name. No one knows the secret.

Do you want to know what became of Our Lady's picture? One day there was a grand procession to Tepeyac Hill. Crowds of people were there. The Indians came dressed in bright beads and gorgeous feathers. Our Lady's picture was in the procession, too. She was going to have a place above the altar in church. Everyone prayed and sang. God's dear Mother must have been pleased. And she let them know it.

Some Indians began a bow and arrow stunt for Our Lady. By accident one Indian boy was shot. He lay dead. They carried him near to the picture and begged Mary to help. And right off he came to life. Not even a scar was left where the arrow had struck. All the people fell on their knees to thank their Mother. From that time she has listened to their prayers and helped them. Didn't she promise that? (Comments.)

Mexicans are not satisfied with having the blessed picture just in church. It is on beds, on furniture, on houses, and even on cars. Every day crowds go to the church to pray to their merciful Mother. And they don't walk up the aisles. They go up on their knees. (Comments.)

Can you tell me what country you live in? Yes, and it is in North America. And so is Mexico. So Guadalupe is Queen of all America. She belongs to us, too.

Now just think, Mary appeared like an Indian. She came to a very poor Indian. There must have been something she liked about him. Where was he going on the Saturday she came on the hill? Yes, and Mary knows that Mass is the most wonderful thing in the world. She loves the Mass. John loved it, too. And that's why Mary thought so much of him. (Comments.)

Remember this: John had been a poor pagan. But he listened to the missionaries and was baptized a Catholic. He was very big when that happened. And then he had to wait a while for his First Communion. How he tried to get his heart ready for that day! See what a fine Catholic he turned out to be. It looks as if he was always saying yes to God and Our Lady. *And how much he loved Mary and the Mass.* (Write these two words on the chalkboard.)

We little Marys and Marios are thinking hard about those two words, aren't we? We shall love the Mass better. Mary will help us. (Consecration.)

### Suggested Reading

"The Grace of Guadalupe" by Frances P. Keyes: Julian Messner, New York.

"Our Lady of America" by Rev. G. L. Lee: J. Murphy & Co., New York.

"Roses for Mexico" by Ethel C. Eliot: Macmillan Co., New York.

"Shrines of Our Lady" by Sister Mary Jean Dorsey: Sheed & Ward, New York.

CHAPTER XIV

## MARY'S LITTLE MOHAWK

*First Talk*

Maybe you would like to have another Indian story. This time it is about a little papoose. Her real name was Tekakwitha. But her mother liked to call her Star Blossom.

This pretty name did not make her mother happy. Each day she felt sadder and sadder. Star Blossom was not christened.

**MARY'S LITTLE MOHAWK**

Bright Dawn (that was her mother) was a Christian. But the father was a pagan. He was the powerful Chief of the village. Everyone was afraid of him, even Bright Dawn. Now you know why the baby was not christened. (Comments.)

One evening the mother was singing a lullaby to her little one.

Close your eyes, my lit- tle pa- poose
The bird- ies have gone to their nests;
Squir- rels are peep-ing to see if you're sleep- ing,
To see how my lit- tle one rests.

Bright Dawn sang it over and over very softly. At last the little papoose was in dreamland. Then the mother kissed her baby and whispered, "My poor little one, I hope. . . ." She did not finish. Right behind her stood the Chief. "I heard your whisper, Bright Dawn. Why is she poor? She is the daughter of a powerful Chief. What more do you want? Speak!" He almost shouted.

The poor mother did not dare to look up. She said, "Oh, Strong Pine, I would love to have the blessed water poured on Star Blossom's head."

Strong Pine looked at her for a moment. "Never, never!" he screamed. "I have spoken." And off he tramped.

Bright Dawn knelt beside her child. She folded her hands and prayed, "O Great White Manitou (explain) hear my words, and send a Blackrobe to baptize my child, Star Blossom." (Comments.)

Think of all the pagan babies who are not baptized. Can we help? Yes, and by buying babies we can be thanking God for our own Baptism. Let us thank God right now for that grace. (Consecration.)

## Second Talk

What did we thank God for in our last story? Let us see what is going to happen in this one.

Star Blossom was growing up very fast. Everyone in the village loved her. Even Strong Pine was very fond of her. She could make the big Chief smile whenever she wanted.

A day came when there was great trouble in the village. The Indians were getting a terrible virus called smallpox. Very few got better. In a few days Chief Strong Pine, little Brother, and Bright Dawn were dead. Poor little Star Blossom got the fever, too. She got over it. But she had no one left, and she was only five.

In the village there lived a Christian squaw. All the Indians called her Good Squaw. She was kind to everyone. She had been a friend to Bright Dawn. They used to talk together about God and Our Lady. Good Squaw loved little Star Blossom. So she took the child to her lodge. She was like another mother to the lonesome little girl. Every day the child would beg for stories about the heavenly Queen who lived with God.

One day Star Blossom's uncle came to the lodge. He was dressed like her father had been. He said to her, "I am Chief White Eagle now. You must come to my lodge. I will keep you. Good Squaw must give you to me." The squaw felt very bad, but the child felt worse. Tears came into the girl's eyes. Good Squaw whispered, "A Chief's daughter must never cry." Then she whispered, "Do not forget about God. Pray to the heavenly Queen. Some day the Blackrobe will come. He will pour the blessed water on your head."

The little Indian girl went with her uncle. Her stepmother did not like her. She left all the hard work for Tekakwitha. That's what they always called her now.

Do you think Tekakwitha forgot about God? (Comments.) No, indeed. She prayed very often every day. And she often thought of Our Lady. She was getting big now. And she was always willing to help others. Everyone loved her except her step-mother. Tekakwitha loved everyone but she did not copy any of their pagan sins. All she wanted was to be a child of God.

Good Squaw met Tekakwitha in the forest one day. She said, "Dear child, I am going away to the Christian village. I cannot stay with these bad pagans. Do what I told you and some day you will be God's child." Before Tekakwitha could say a word, Good Squaw was gone.

Now the poor girl had no one to go to. (Comments.)

Soon after that she heard that the Blackrobe was

coming. So she kept on obeying her stepmother and praying. And she never had a sad face.

Who was Tekakwitha acting like? Yes, but she didn't know it. And all the while Our Lady must have been pleased with her. I know many little children who are pleasing to Our Lady. Who do you think they are? (Comments.) Let us say our consecration and mean every word.

## Third Talk

What good news did Tekakwitha hear? Well, very soon the Blackrobe came. The few Christians in the village were happy about it. But the pagans were not. And one of these was Chief White Eagle.

The Blackrobe met Tekakwitha in the forest one morning. Because he was so kind she told him all about herself. She asked him to baptize her. The Blackrobe told her to ask her uncle first. So Tekakwitha prayed and then she went to the Chief. And guess what? He said yes. The happy girl could hardly believe it.

When do you think she was baptized? On Easter! Now she was God's child. And now she was Mary's child, too. She took the new name, Katherine. She spent that Easter day thanking God. She made a whole lot of sacrifices, too. That was to show God that she meant what she said. (Comments.)

From then on she did not work on Sunday anymore. All the pagan Indians made fun of her. Her stepmother said that if she did not work she would not get anything to eat. But Katherine smiled and made the sacrifice. (Comments.)

Katherine had been used to praying in the forest. It was quiet there. And it was easy to talk to God in a quiet place. But now it was different. The Blackrobe had built a little church. The Indian girl loved to go there because our Lord was there. At Christmas it was wonderful. There was a crib and on the straw lay the Saviour, so little and so poor. And right beside Him was His lovely Mother. The Indians came in crowds to look and look. They stayed and stayed. And you could hear them singing the same hymn over and over. All this made Katherine so happy. But it made the pagan Indians angry.

Soon Katherine began to wish for a better place to live. She thought of Good Squaw living in the Christian village. So she spoke to the Blackrobe about it. He told her to pray and wait. She said, "I shall help my stepmother all I can. I shall pray more than ever. The beautiful Lady and her Baby Son will listen to me."

What was Katherine going to do? And Who were going to listen to her? Was she right about that? How do we know that Mary listens? (Comments.)

Let us fold our hands and say our consecration so that she will be glad to listen.

*Fourth Talk*

(Picture of Blessed Katherine.)

What made Katherine so happy in our last story?

Well, at last the Blackrobe told her she could go away. The plans were all made. Her cousin and another Christian Indian were to take her. They would have to paddle through many rivers.

White Eagle had to go to another village. Her stepmother had gone to gather berries. So the Blackrobe told Katherine, "Now is the time. You must go today." The poor girl was terribly frightened. Katherine slipped away quietly with the two Indians.

But White Eagle got home that same day. And was he angry when they told him that Katherine had run away! He started off to the forest and had almost caught up with her. The poor girl prayed to Our Lady and hid under some bushes. The other two Indians did not get a chance to hide. But they played a trick on the Chief. The first one began cutting the bark of a tree. And the other one sat against a tree and began to smoke. White Eagle came close to them. He said to himself, "These Indians don't look as if they are running away. I guess I came too late to catch the ones I want. They were too quick for me." And back he went to the village.

When all danger was over, Katherine and her friends started off again. When they reached the Christian village, Good Squaw was there to meet them. She was as happy as Katherine.

When the happy girl met the Blackrobe, she told him how much she wanted Holy Communion, He said, "Pray, my child, and we shall see." The Indians had to wait a long time for that Sacrament. The priests wanted to be sure that they really stopped being pagans.

Then one day the priest told Katherine that she could receive our Lord. How do you think she got ready? (Comments.) Yes, and those are just the things you little Marys and Marios are doing, aren't they?

Everyone in the village loved Katherine. And of course they were happy about her First Communion. They watched her pray when she had our Lord in her heart. Many Indians said it was good to be near her. People could pray better. Isn't that a lovely thing to say about a person? Our Lady would like all of us to be that way.

Shortly after her Communion, Katherine was consecrated to Our Lady. From then on she copied Our Lady more and more. She gave up the beautiful beaded bands she wore, as a sacrifice. Then she gave away her lovely red blanket that she liked so much. And ever after that she wore a blue one to make her think of Mary.

Some time later Katherine got too sick to work any more. She couldn't even go to church. So she said to her angel, "You go to Mass for me. Bring me back the graces. I don't want to miss one of them." I guess she knew what we know about the Mass. Who can tell me what that is? (Comments.)

A day came when Katherine was dying. The priest brought her Holy Communion. All the Indians turned out and followed the priest to the poor little place. They knelt on the ground outside and prayed. A few days later the dear girl died. Now she had never been pretty. Her skin had been spotted by the smallpox. But all of a sudden the dead girl's face changed. She looked like a beautiful angel.

The Indians came in crowds to look at her and kiss

her hands. They begged her to pray for them. And now our dear Katherine Tekakwitha is in heaven with our Lord and the Heavenly Queen. And here is a lovely surprise for all the little Marys and Marios. The Holy Father in Rome has declared her *Blessed* Katherine Tekakwitha. So, we can now pray to her as *Blessed Katherine.*

How did Katherine copy Mary? (Comments.) Let us say our consecration the way Katherine would have said it.

### Suggested Reading

"Treasure of the Mohawks" by Teri Martini: St. Anthony Guild Press, Paterson, N.J.

"Catherine Tekakwitha" by Daniel Sargent: Longmans, Green Co., New York.

"Drums of Destiny" by William Sanbourg: Grail Publications, St. Meinrad, Indiana.

"Kateri of the Mohawks" by Marie C. Buerhle: Bruce Pub. Co., Milwaukee, Wis.

CHAPTER XV

## MARY'S HOUSE

*First Talk*

(Picture of Our Lady.)

Let children comment on the picture. I wonder if we ever think about how much Our Lady has done for us and for everyone else.

Remember the Christmas story? Who came over the hills that night to see the Little Saviour? When Joseph brought them in, how did they look? Yes, very poor and maybe not too clean. Did Mary say, "Don't

**MARY'S HOUSE**

bring those people in here." Oh, no! She was glad they came. And I am sure she let them touch the Holy Child. And maybe she told them to stay as long as they wanted.

You see, Mary knew why Jesus came down on earth. It was to help and save people. He loved all kinds of people. When she was kind to the shepherds, she was copying Jesus.

One day Mary carried her Baby to the Temple. She wanted to offer the Heavenly Father a gift. The Gift was Jesus. While she was there an old man came in. He had asked God to let him live to see the Saviour. And sure enough, here was the Child in the Mother's arms. The old man knew it right off. He went up to Mary. Very sweetly she laid her Baby in the old man's arms. He looked at the dear Mother. Then he said, "Some will love this Child. Some will not love Him. You will feel very bad about it. It will always hurt your heart like a sword."

Mary never forgot that. But she did not stop loving people. No, she just kept on praying for all of us. You and me and everybody. Why?

Our Lady watched Jesus grow up. She watched Him help Joseph. And when Saint Joseph died, she saw her Big Boy take charge of the carpenter shop. He often told His Mother that some day He must leave her. He had to let the people know Who He was. He must teach them the way to heaven, too. Mary listened, and she knew He would do something very hard for all of us. (Comments.) And don't you think her heart ached?

But we must remember that Mary was copying Jesus. It made her happy to think He would save souls from hell. So she offered all her heartaches to God.

Can we ever thank Mary enough? What is the best way to thank her? Yes, and those sacrifices will be a lovely surprise. (Consecration.)

*Second Talk*

(Suitable picture.)

What made Mary sad in the last story? (Comments.)

Well, the day came at last. Jesus kissed Mary good-bye. She watched Him go down the road.

Mary said to herself, "I had Him with me a long time. Now I am glad to share Him with others. He will tell them about heaven. He will do wonderful things, too. And the people will surely believe. They will believe He is God."

But Mary did not always know what was coming. She heard how some people loved our Lord. And she heard how others hated Him. At last she heard that they wanted to kill Him.

And then one day she heard that the soldiers had taken Him. The wicked priests and the rough mob were treating Him very badly. Mary stood at the street corner with John the Apostle. She wanted to watch and listen. In a few minutes the mob came along. There was her dear Son. A terrible cross was on His shoulders. He fell under it. Mary could not get close to Him, but they looked at one another. They both felt very sad.

Mary and John followed Jesus. Some holy friends of Mary went along. After some time, Mary got near the awful Cross. She heard our Lord say, "Father, forgive them." And in her heart she said the same thing. Then she heard our Lord talk to the thief on the cross next to him. He said, "This day you shall be with Me in Paradise." Mary was glad for the poor thief. You see, she wants everyone to get to heaven. That's why she made so many sacrifices for us. And that's why she prays so much for us. (Comments.)

Then at three o'clock our dear Lord died. Afterwards they took Him down from the Cross. They laid Him on Mary's lap. She kissed His wounds. But she did not fuss or scold. She just thought, "I hope all this will do bad people a lot of good. I am sure it will make them better. And it will make good ones holier."

Very soon Jesus was laid in the tomb. Mary and the others had to go home. How lonesome Our Lady was! She suffered a lot, didn't she? (Comments.) It was all for you and for me.

When we look at the Cross remember this. Mary shared in the hard time Jesus had. That is why our Lord lets her hand us all the graces we need.

Let us thank Our lady for all she suffered. We shall say our consecration now just to please her Immaculate Heart.

*Third Talk*

(Suitable picture.)

How was Our Lady in the last story? But we know that our dear Saviour came back to life again. He arose from the dead on the third day. That was the first Easter.

Now whom did He go to see first? Yes, indeed. He could not keep her waiting any longer. How happy Mary was when she saw Him. (Comments.)

Our Lord stayed on earth for forty days. But only His friends could see Him. Then one day He went up into heaven. Mary saw Him go up. Who else saw Him go? When He was gone, who took care of the Apostles? Yes, she stayed with them as much as she could. They told her all about their troubles. She gave them good advice. (Explain advice.) So God's first priests all went to Mary. And I think she prayed a lot for them, too. After a while they went off to different places to teach people about our Lord. But when they came back they went straight to Our Lady. One day they all came at once except Thomas. They found Mary very tired out. And while they were there she said goodbye to them. Then she closed her eyes and went to heaven. You see Jesus wanted His dear Mother up there. How do you think the Apostles felt? (Comments.)

After Mary was buried, along came Thomas. Poor Thomas cried. He wanted to see Mary's face once more. So the Apostles took him to her tomb. Peter opened the tomb. It was filled with roses and lilies. But Mary was not there. Then they knew God had taken His Mother, body and soul, into heaven. That must have been a wonderful day in heaven. (Comments.)

Now we believe that she is the Queen of Heaven,

don't we? Well, what does a queen wear on her head? I wonder who put the crown on her. Yes, and wasn't our Lord glad to crown His own dear Mother?

But we are not afraid of the Queen of Heaven, are we? Oh, no, we love her. She is a merciful mother. She listens to her children's prayers. And how does she treat little Marys and Marios? Yes, she loves them dearly. Suppose we give our Queen some extra surprises today. (Let children suggest.) (Consecration.)

*Fourth Talk*

(Suitable picture.)

Remember the trip we took with Mary and Joseph? Well, we shall take another one. We shall go to Nazareth. We want to see the little house where the heavenly Queen lived.

All right, let's close our eyes. Don't open until I say so. Now we start off. And here we are in Nazareth. We walk down the hill. Ah, there is the holy house. How small it is! And we think Jesus, Mary, and Joseph lived there.

But something is happening. The house is moving. It is going up into the air. Angels are holding on to it. They are steering it behind the hill. Now it is out of sight. It is gone. Open your eyes. (Comments.)

Do you think that really happened? No? Well, it did. That holy house was in Nazareth for years and years. People from all over came to see it. Priests said Mass in it.

Then one day the holy house was lifted out of the ground. Up it went. Angels were holding it. And off it sailed. Many people watched it, but they could not stop it. They just looked and looked until it disappeared. Guess what happened to it? (Comments.)

That holy house was set down in another country. People saw it coming. They watched it come down quietly and rest on the ground. Crowds began to come. Many miracles happened to those who prayed there. So at last a beautiful church was built all around it. The holy house fits in a corner of the big church. Many priests say Mass there in the holy little house.

It is called the Holy House of Loreto. That is the name of the place where the angels placed it. So our Lord must have loved that House. I wonder why? (Comments.)

We can't go to the Holy House. But we can go to the One who made that house holy. Who was That? Yes, and where does He live now? So when we look at the Tabernacle we can remember this. Jesus lives here. And Our Lady will love to see her little Marys and Marios visit Him in this House on the Altar. (Consecration.)

### Suggested Reading

"Shrines of Our Lady Around the World" by Zsolt Aradi: Farrar, Straus & Cudahy, New York.

"Our Lady of Loreto" by Father Gilbert, O.F.M.: Franciscan Annals, The Friary, Olton, Birmingham, England.

"Shrines of Our Lady" by Sister Mary Jean Dorsey: Sheed & Ward, New York.

"Loreto (Santa Casa)," Catholic Encyclopedia, Vol. 13, p. 454.

# CHAPTER XVI

## MARY'S PICTURE

*First Talk*

If you were up in heaven, would you want to come down here any more? But because Mary loves to help us she has come down lots of times. She came to Bernadette. The place was Lourdes.

Mary had something to tell Bernadette. Our dear Lady knew that many people were getting very bad. God was going to punish them. So Mary said to Bernadette, "Penance, penance." You see, when we do penance we punish ourselves for our sins. And we can do penance for other people, too. Then God does not have to punish. And that was what our dear Mother wanted. And it is so important that she came from heaven to tell it to Bernadette. (Comments.)

Our Lady had another thing to tell us! When Bernadette asked, "Who are you?" Mary looked up to heaven and said, "I am the Immaculate Conception." We can say that another way, "Mary, conceived without sin." It is on our medals. So she told us her loveliest name. Besides all that, Mary had something to give. Well, she told Bernadette to scrape the dirt from the ground. Bernadette did. And a spring of clear water began to flow out. That water is still coming from the rock this very day. Many sick people have been cured by that wonderful water. Our Lord does many miracles for His dear Mother, doesn't He?

Then, later on, our sweet Mother came to Fatima. I think we know that story. But there is one thing I

**MARY'S PICTURE**

did not tell you. Besides asking for sacrifice and the Rosary, Our Lady told the children to have processions. She likes processions. She likes the hymns and prayers. So when you are in a procession, you know that it is pleasing to your heavenly Mother. You know she is looking and listening. And of course the main thing about Fatima is this. If we do what Our Lady wants, Russia will stop being bad to other countries. Russia will turn to God. And we shall have peace.

Mary told us this so that we would be safe. Mary never gets tired of helping us, does she? (Comments.) We shall say our consecration to please her Immaculate Heart.

*Second Talk*

Our Lady made another visit to this world. You see she is busy thinking of her children down here. Well, this time she came to someone whose name begins with D. (Comments.) And she gave him something we all use. (Comments.)

The Rosary helped him, didn't it? It put an end to the bad ideas of the heretics. It helps us, too. And so many of you say the family Rosary. Our Lady must be very happy about it.

Did you know that the Rosary is a crown? A crown of prayers for Our Lady. She told our dear little friends at Fatima that she was the Queen of the Rosary. Now when we think of a queen we think of a crown, too. So that will help you to remember that your prayers on the beads make a crown for our Queen. And what does the first part of the word Rosary say? Then the prayers on your beads make a crown of roses for our Queen.

One time our Blessed Mother came down at night. She came to a person whose name began with C. The person had another name. It began with a Z. (Comments.) She gave her something you wear. And what is it called? That was another gift from our kind Mother. Tell me something you remember of the Medal story. (Comments.)

Mary came to many places. But they were far away over the ocean. Did she ever come to America? I am glad you remembered. What did she ask for? And what did she give us? Yes, she had given us her Rosary and her medal. So then she thought it would be nice to give us her picture.

Mary told John something that we made into slogans. Does anyone remember? Very well, Karen. Mary is a merciful Mother. She listens to all prayers. I think you should tell others those things about Mary. You will make people love her. And Mary will love you more for doing that.

Just think, our heavenly Queen has come down from her throne to help us. She could have said, "I am not going to bother about people any more. My Son has done enough for them." But our Mother could never think that way. She always copies our Lord. She thinks the way He thinks. She wants us to remember the question, "Why did God make you?" Let us say the answer together.

That is just what Mary wants for each of us. Isn't she a wonderful Mother? That's why she bothers so much about us. Let us make our consecration to our good Mother.

*Third Talk*

(Have a picture of St. Simon receiving the scapular.)

Did you ever hear of anyone named Simon? Well, once there was a very holy priest by that name. Now he is St. Simon.

Father Simon went walking in the garden one day. He loved to look at the flowers. Somehow they made him think of our Blessed Mother. He often thought that Mary was the loveliest flower in heaven.

The chapel was close to the garden. So, after a while, Father Simon slipped into the chapel for a visit. He was still thinking of Mary. What was that soft sound he heard? He raised his eyes. There before him was Our Lady with many, many angels. She smiled at him. Then she offered him something she held in her hand. (Show the picture.) Mary then told Simon something very special. She said that those who die wearing her scapular shall not go to hell. So the scapular is surely something very special and important, isn't it? We call that Mary's scapular promise. (Comments.)

But Mary wants to do more for souls. She wants to help souls even in Purgatory. You know she is Queen of Purgatory. So she goes there and takes souls to heaven. And if you wear the scapular so much the better. So Mary helps us when we are living. She helps us when we are dying. And she helps us in Purgatory.

What a kind heavenly Mother we have. I hope you

will not forget about her this summer. Be sure you wear your scapular. You know the whole story about it now. And be sure you wear the other gift Mary gave us, her Miraculous Medal. Say your consecration often. You know you are little Marys and Marios. And Our Lady knows it, too. She will be looking and listening.

Let us see how many slogans we can remember. (Have children repeat those they can recall.) Maybe we can tell other children about Mary. Maybe we can tell them some slogans. And all the while Our Lady will be smiling down on us. She will be getting special graces for us. We shall say our consecration now and make her smile.

*Fourth Talk*

(Picture of Our Lady of Good Counsel.)

One day a large crowd of people was going to a fair. They were dressed in their best. And they were having a happy time. On the way, they had to pass a church that was half-built. Just as they got near it, they heard lovely music. But it wasn't coming from the church. Everyone looked toward the sky. That is where the beautiful sounds were coming from.

All of a sudden the people saw a little cloud coming toward them. It looked like silver. Down, down it sailed very slowly. At that moment all the church bells in the town rang out by themselves. The cloud came nearer. Something was on the cloud. In a few minutes the people saw what it was. A beautiful picture of Mary holding her Child. The cloud was gone.

But the picture went into the half-built church. It

placed itself on the highest wall and stayed there. The people forgot about the fair. Instead, they crowded into the church. And there they stayed all night praying and singing before the holy picture.

Someone said, "Maybe the picture will fall, and then we won't have it." So they looked to see if it were safe. But they found that the picture touched the wall in one little spot. That was down at the lefthand corner. And no one could move it from that spot. The rest of the picture did not even touch the wall. That was years ago. And it is still in the same place. Jesus and Mary must have liked the place very much because many miracles have happened there.

Would you like to see a picture of it? Well, here it is. (Comments.) Jesus is telling Mary something, isn't He? Mary always knew just what to do because Jesus told her. That's why she can give us good advice if we ask her. Do you know what advice means? We can call her Our Lady of Good Advice. The real name is Our Lady of Good Counsel. Counsel is the same as advice.

Do you think you will need good advice during vacation? Yes, all little Marys and Marios will need it. You just have to say this little prayer. Our Lady of Good Advice, tell me what to do.

We shall need advice about where to play. Advice about the right kind of playmates. About remembering your prayers. About getting to Mass on Sundays and on Mary's holyday in August. And about getting to Confession and Communion just as carefully as we went the first time. So we shall ask Mary for advice, and say a big yes to her right away.

Mary has done so much for us. It would be very sad if we let our vacation make us bad. But that isn't going to happen, is it? We won't forget our slogans either. (Comments.)

So we shall keep close to Mary's Immaculate Heart all summer. Then we shall be close to our Lord. (Consecration.)

### Suggested Reading

"Our Lady of Good Counsel" by Thos. C. Middleton: Catholic Encyclopedia, Vol. XI, p. 361.

"Listen, Mother of God!" by Rev. Hugh Blunt: Catholic Literary Guild, Ozone Park, New York.

"Shrines of Our Lady" by Zsolt Aradi: Farrar, Straus & Cudahy, New York.

"The Secret of Mary Explained to Children," Montfort Publications, Bay Shore, N.Y.

unnecessarily. But in a river or a narrow channel it was often necessary to tack every few minutes, with the whole crew on full alert.

The helm or steering wheel was supervised by a petty officer known as a quartermaster, and with up to four men doing the physical work of moving, as conditions demanded. Two could stand on each side of the wheel, and it was double, with one wheel behind the other. The leading helmsman was forward on the weather side, where the wind was coming from. The rate at which the ship would turn depended on the ship's size and speed, but often it would be at least several seconds before the effect of moving the wheel was visible, as the ship's head began to move against the horizon. In a tight corner the captain or the officer of the watch might give orders such as 'hard-a-port' or 'steady as she goes' direct to the helmsman or quarter-master. At other times, the helmsman might be ordered to head for a particular object, such as a lighthouse or landmark, or a ship if they were part of the fleet. Out of sight of land, he would be instructed to steer a compass course. There were two compasses in a wooden box known as a binnacle just in front of him, one on each side of the wheel, with a light between them for use at night. Each was divided into the four cardinal points, north, south, east and west. These were subdivided into north-east, south-west and so on, and then into east-north-east etc., and finally into subdivisions such as north by east and north-east by north. At other times, the ship might have an unfavourable wind and the helmsman would be ordered to steer as close to it as possible – full and by, sailing by the wind but keeping the sails full. This was the most skilled task, for if he went too close to the wind the ship would begin to lose speed, the sails would begin to rustle and the ship would be taken aback and in some danger.

A warship usually carried six to eight boats, stowed on booms in the waist of the ship, or hung from davits over the side. They were not lifeboats in the modern sense of the term, for they did not have extra buoyancy to keep them afloat in the worst conditions, but they could be used if the ship sank, or to rescue a man who fell into the water. Mostly they were used for transport, carrying goods and stores to and from the ship. If the winds were light or unfavourable, the boats could tow the ship, or they could lay an anchor out ahead so that men at the capstan could haul the ship up to it. Sometimes they were armed with light guns or carronades. They could be used to land sailors or troops on a friendly or enemy shore, or in cutting-out expeditions, capturing enemy ships in harbour.

All boats could be either rowed or sailed, but some were better at one than the other. Pinnaces and barges were long, narrow boats, mostly used to row officers ashore or from one ship to another. Cutters and jolly-boats were wide-hulled with sharp bows, and were good for sailing and in rough seas. Launches and longboats were of heavy construction, for carrying anchors, guns or heavy stores. Each boat had a regular crew, headed either by a young midshipman or by a coxswain, who was a petty officer. The captain's coxswain was in a trusted position, often the captain's main link with the lower deck and one of his principal servants who would follow him from ship to ship.

The master was the main navigating officer of the ship, though all the commissioned officers were expected to have some knowledge of navigation. At first the master had to supply his own charts, but in 1795 the Admiralty Hydrographic Department was formed and packs of charts were issued for particular areas. But a warship would often have to operate where little charting had been done, and the master could not always rely on what was available. At the Battle of the Nile, Captain Foley of the *Goliath* used a French chart of Aboukir Bay to find a way round the head of the enemy line, to great effect.

There were four main ways of navigating a ship, according to circumstances. In a narrow channel or estuary, pilotage was used. A local pilot might be taken on board, with knowledge of the underwater features of the port, its tides and currents, and the landmarks that could be followed. The task was far easier when there were buoys and beacons to mark the edges of the channels. When at sea but in sight of shore, landmarks were naturally used to the full. There were a few lighthouses, such as the one on the dangerous rocks at Eddystone near Plymouth, and the famous Bell Rock off the Scottish coast was finished in 1811. Prominent features such as churches were marked on the charts and the master could take bearings on them with a compass. With two or more bearings, he would be able to establish the ship's position with a reasonable degree of accuracy, and avoid features like sandbanks and underwater rocks. He could order a seaman to cast the lead over the side to take soundings so that he knew the depth of water under him and could tell if it was beginning to shallow.

When out of sight of land, a navigator might use dead reckoning. He would find the course steered over a period by the compass and the distance travelled by casting the ship's log over the stern. This was a piece of wood attached to a long line with knots in it. It was allowed to run out for a period of time measured by a sandglass, and the number of knots could be used to calculate the speed. The master would also have to allow for tides and winds that might push the ship in one direction or another, so dead reckoning was subject to many errors, and had to be checked by other means as far as possible.

On ocean voyages this was done by astral navigation, using the sun, moon, stars and planets. It was quite easy to find the latitude by measuring the height of the sun at noon each day, and the time of noon could give indication of longitude. This depended on the chronometer, a very accurate clock that was adjusted for variations in climate and temperature and could withstand the hardships of sea service. The navigator used his quadrant or sextant to measure angles very accurately. The sextant was the more accurate of the two, made of brass and using a system of mirrors to allow measurement over a wide angle. It could also be used to measure the distance between the moon and a star, giving an accurate time if a chronometer was not available, but involving a laborious calculation. The master might also take sights of several stars, preferably at dawn or dusk when the horizon was visible. From these he could plot his position very accurately. All this, however, depended on both the sky and the horizon being in sight.

# CHAPTER 6

# War and Battle

The Royal Navy of Nelson's time had more than its share of action against the enemy. It fought six great fleet battles (three under Nelson himself) and won them all. It captured 570 enemy warships between 1793 and 1802 and many thousands of merchant ships. As well as the great battles, it fought many 'single-ship' actions when one frigate confronted another, and, except against the Americans, it could expect to prevail unless the enemy ship was more than 50 per cent bigger. The most notable of all was when in 1801 Thomas Cochrane, in the tiny brig *Speedy* with only fourteen light guns, took the Spanish *Gamo* with more than four times the crew and gun power. The navy supported amphibious landings in Egypt, South Africa, the West Indies, Ceylon and many other places. It maintained the Duke of Wellington's army during its successful campaign in Spain and Portugal.

But most of the navy's work was routine and often boring. It escorted huge convoys of merchant ships to maintain Britain's supply lines. It patrolled the seas to look for the enemy, and, most important of all, it blockaded the great enemy fleets in their ports, so that they could not intervene in the sea war without risking battle. According to the American naval strategist Alfred Thayer Mahan, 'Those far distant, storm-beaten ships upon which the Grand Army never looked, stood between it and the dominion of the world.' The blockade off the principal French port of Brest was maintained throughout most of the wars, though conditions were rough in the Atlantic waters. The action attracted little prestige, and Seaman William Robinson found that they got the nickname 'Channel

gropers' from the girls in port. Nelson kept up a
blockade off the Mediterranean port of Toulon for two
years from 1803 to 1805, until the French finally broke
out. Cadiz was blockaded by Admiral Jervis in the
1790s, until he beat the Spanish at the Battle of Cape
St Vincent and took the title of his earldom from the
site of the battle. When the combined French and
Spanish fleets unwisely left Cadiz in October 1805,
Nelson was able to crush them at the Battle of
Trafalgar.

Warships, especially frigates, also engaged in single-
ship action, the staple of maritime fiction. This took
place when two ships of approximately equal strength
met on the oceans and fought it out. Such encounters
tended to be highly publicised, and it was a great
shock when war with the United States began in
1812, and British frigates began to lose to American
ships of nominally equal force.

Capturing ships, or taking prizes as it was known,
was the most satisfying part of a seaman's career.

By law the value of the prize was divided between the captors, with the lion's share going to the officers. A popular cartoon shows a ship going into action at Trafalgar, with one of the crew praying that the enemy shot be divided in the same proportion as the prize money. An admiral was entitled to one-eighth of the value, whether he was present or not – thus Admiral Keith became rich from the capture of Ceylon, though he was miles away at the time. A captain got a quarter to himself, and so his fortunes could be transformed if he were given a 'cruise' – an expedition to raid enemy merchant ships. Captain Wentworth in Jane Austen's *Persuasion* is a far better marriage prospect after he has gained £20,000 in this way. At the other end of the scale, the seamen might make sums in tens or occasionally hundreds of pounds.

The prize money system might encourage captains to concentrate on enemy merchant ships, which often carried valuable cargoes and were less likely to fight back than warships. The authorities did several things to prevent this. After a great victory such as Trafalgar, Parliament usually voted a sum of money to be divided among the fleet. And honours such as promotions, medals, knighthoods and peerages were only given after successful actions against warships.

For fighting purposes, the ship was divided into a number of gun crews. Each was a cross-section of the whole crew, with skilled men in charge and unskilled landsmen, marines and boys for the heavier or more menial tasks. A 32-pounder, the largest gun in common service, had a crew of seven, but in most cases only one side of the ship would be fighting at once, so two crews could combine. Around the time of Trafalgar, the seventh gun on the lower deck of HMS *Bellerophon* was captained by James Marshall, from Waterford in Ireland, who was the oldest man in the ship at 56 and had served seventeen years in the Newfoundland trade and thirteen in the Royal Navy. He had a fellow Irishman to assist him and an American negro, John Hatchett, who was probably an escaped slave. There was also a French royalist who had been pressed from a merchant ship in 1794, a brazier from Bristol who had spent five years at sea, and a shoemaker from Cambridge who had only gone to sea at the age of 42. One or two marines were probably attached to the gun as well, to help carry powder. They could be called away to use their muskets in close action. In many ships boys were used to handle the powder.

Captain Riou gave detailed orders on how to operate the 18-pounders of the *Amazon*. There would be silence after the men were called to their quarters, 'so that when a loud and general order comes from the mouth of the captain every man may hear and comprehend'. Assuming a crew of ten, Nos 1, 3 and 5 would stand with the gun tackle on one side ready to haul the gun out as necessary, with Nos 2, 4 and 6 on the other side – the story that the traditional order 'Two-six heave' was based on the arrangement of the gun crew is pure myth. Meanwhile No. 8, the captain of the gun, would stand by the train tackle which stopped the gun from running out through its port with the rolling of the ship. No. 1 would put the gunpowder cartridge into the muzzle, followed by a shot and a wad of rope to keep it in place. No. 2 would ram them home and the rest of the crew hauled the gun out. No. 10 stood behind the gun to supply the different types of shot that might be needed, including solid round shot, grape and canister. Behind him was No. 9, a boy who handled the powder in canvas or paper cartridges.

As a ship sailed into battle, there were mixed feelings among officers and men. Officers often thought about the possibilities of prize money and promotion, but one young midshipman wrote as he sailed into action at Trafalgar, 'Should I, my dear parents, fall in defence of my king, let that thought console you. I feel not the least dread in my spirits.' One officer overheard men in a gun crew as they sailed into the Battle of the Nile:

There are thirteen sail of the line, and a whacking lot of frigates and small craft. I think we'll hammer the rust off ten of them, if not the whole boiling . . . I'm glad we have twigged them at last, I want some new rigging d-bly for Sundays and mustering days . . . Well, mind your eye, we'll be at it 'hammer and tongs' directly. I have rammed three shot besides a round of grape in my gun. Damme, I'll play hell and turn up Jack amongst them.

Nelson heard a similar conversation in his flagship *Vanguard* and remarked, 'I knew what stuff I had under me.' But at the same battle, John Nicoll, part of the crew of the *Goliath*, saw that underneath the jollity there was 'a serious cast' on the faces of the men, though 'not a shade of doubt or fear'.

The admiral decided the tactics of the battle. There were two important things to remember. Firstly, the ships on both sides were entirely dependent on the wind and he had to make the best use of it.

In conventional naval tactics he would try to get the 'weather gage', that is, to get his ships to the windward side of the enemy. This would allow him to choose the range of the fight, when and where to attack the enemy line, and it would blow the gun smoke towards the enemy to obscure his view.

The second point was that practically all this gun power, and that of the enemy, was on the sides of his ships, very little firing forwards or aft. Even worse, the stern was very weak, and decorated with windows and galleries for the officers. In old-fashioned tactics he would keep his ships in a single line, allowing the maximum use of his gun power and protecting the stern of each ship, except the last in the line. If attacking a single ship, he would try to get under her stern, to rake her with gunfire that passed along the decks, dismounting guns and creating carnage.

In the decades before Nelson, it had been customary for each fleet to form a rigid line of battle and fight it out at quite long range, which rarely produced a decisive result. Already by 1760, admirals were beginning to find more aggressive tactics, exploiting the British seaman's superior seamanship and gunnery – the result of greater practice. At Trafalgar, Nelson's ships sailed towards the enemy line in two columns and broke through it. After that, each captain was on his own. According to Nelson, 'no captain can do very wrong if he places his ship alongside that of an enemy'. He would try to rake the enemy, then attack his weak stern with his own heavy broadside. Failing that, two ships might fight side by side until one or the other surrendered, or was perhaps attacked by a ship on its other side.

As he approached the enemy, the captain needed some members of his crew to trim the sails, and perhaps called one or two men away from each gun for this purpose. But it could be dangerous, since after the action was joined, men became absorbed in the fighting and were reluctant to leave their guns. At the Battle of the Nile, Captain Hallowell of the *Swiftsure*

made certain that his ship was fully anchored and
made ready before he allowed his guns to fire, because
he was 'aware of the difficulty of breaking the men off
from their guns once they have begun to use them'.
At Trafalgar, one young officer was sent below to get
marines to join the party on the upper deck, but he
found it almost impossible and as he said many years
later, 'I need not inform a seaman of the difficulty of
separating a man from his gun.' It was this fanaticism,
rather than any skill at aiming, that gave the British
ships their superiority against the French, Dutch and
Spanish. In 1812, at war with the young United States
Navy, captains like Phillip Broke quickly had to adopt
new tactics to fire more accurately at longer ranges.

Young Louis Roteley describes his experience of
the decks of the *Victory* at Trafalgar:

A man should witness a battle in a three-decker
from the middle-deck, for it beggars all description.
It bewilders the senses of sight and hearing. There

was fire from above, fire from below, besides the fire from the deck I was upon, the guns recoiling with violent reports louder than thunder, the deck heaving and the side straining. I fancied myself in the infernal regions, where every man appeared a devil. Lips might move, but orders and hearing were out of the question: everything was done by signs.

Casualties were high in a great battle, especially among men on the upper decks who were most exposed, and Nelson himself fell at Trafalgar, to be taken below to the cockpit, where he died.

At the Battle of Camperdown eight years earlier there was a shortage of skilled medical staff and so the surgeon of the *Ardent* had to work alone.

Ninety wounded were brought down during the action. The whole cockpit, deck, cabins, wing berths and part of the cable tier, together with my platform and my preparations for dressing were covered with them. So that for a time they were laid on each other at the foot of the ladder where they were brought down ...

Melancholy cries for assistance were addressed to me from every side by wounded and dying, and piteous moans and bewailing from pain and despair. In the midst of these agonising scenes, I was able to preserve myself firm and collected, and embracing in my mind the whole of the situation, to direct my attention where the greatest and most essential services could be performed. Some with wounds, bad indeed and painful, but slight in comparison with the dreadful condition of others, were most vociferous for my assistance.

# CHAPTER 7

# Leaving the Navy

In peacetime a sailor would leave the ship at the end of its voyage or commission, after perhaps two or three years. It was up to him whether he joined another warship, sought work in a merchant ship, or went home with his pay. In wartime he might be transferred from one ship to another and spend many years at sea. Seamen who did not like this tended to desert, despite the difficulties and dangers involved – between 1793 and 1801 alone, 42,000 men ran from the navy out of a fleet that never numbered more than 140,000 men. Leave was often not given to men who seemed likely to desert. Few seamen could swim in those days, and they were not encouraged to do so by officers. Some men would steal boats and row ashore, others would give their officers the slip when in a boat's crew or on shore duty, perhaps with a press gang. They were aided by the fact that there was no police force to track them down, and no certain way of identifying them if they did desert. Some officers kept detailed descriptions of the men, including tattoos – for example, Edward Reilly of HMS *Blake* was 48 years old, 5ft 5½in tall, with dark complexion, dark brown hair, grey eyes and 'stout made'. He came from Belfast and was married. The greatest danger for a deserter was to be pressed into another ship later on, and perhaps come across an officer who knew him. If so, the penalties could be severe, especially if the desertion was compounded by another offence such as theft or assault on an officer. Flogging round the fleet was a common punishment in such cases.

But wars did come to an end eventually, and the remaining men were discharged from the navy, leaving only a small peacetime force. The seaman was paid all his wages, perhaps several years' worth if he had been serving overseas, with prize money added to that. It was then that sailors behaved extravagantly, perhaps buying gold watches and frying them according to one account, or hiring a whole stage coach to take them home. Some were duped by fraudsters, some were elated at the release from naval discipline and spent the bulk of their money in a few days, or were robbed. But some were able to go home with a good deal of money in their pockets and start a new life in peacetime.

For those who did not do well in post-naval life, there was always the prospect of the Royal Naval Hospital at Greenwich. This was a home for retired sailors, built on the orders of Queen Mary in the 1690s and designed by Britain's greatest architect of the age, Christopher Wren. There, sailors would wear a blue uniform, live in dormitories and perhaps earn a little money by telling tourists tales of seafaring and battle.

The others returned home with a little money and a fund of stories, and perhaps enhanced prestige in the seaport towns that many of them came from. Some of the officers had gained fame, wealth, high rank and great honour. Others, such as Lieutenant John Fullarton of Ayrshire, had led mediocre careers. 'Nothing but the common occurrences of services. Health broken from climate and hurts received, like a thousand others upon the active list. As Jack says, "not worth a single damn".'

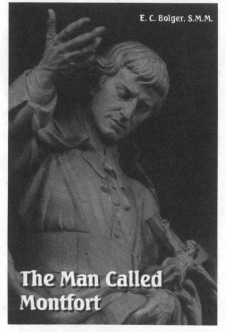